Gateshead
Council

CW00400745

Please visit us at www.gateshead.gov.uk/libraries

County Durham

DH3 4LF

0191 433 6101

05

DUE FOR RETURN	DUE FOR RETURN	DUE FOR RETURN
2 7 2005		
1 0 NOV 2005		
20 Dec 2005		
1 6 SEP 2015		

Please return books by the latest date stamped above. You may be able to renew books that are not reserved by another borrower. Write to us or ring us before the books are overdue, giving the due date and barcode number at the bottom of this page, or log onto our website - ask us for your PIN.

We charge for books not returned by their date due. The current charges are displayed in libraries.

You are responsible for the care and safe keeping of books you have borrowed. Please report any loss or damage promptly.

Please let us know if you change your address or lose your ticket.

DERWENTSIDE
district council
An Environment for Success

Supported by
DURHAM
COUNTY
COUNCIL
a first class county for
Arts, Libraries & Museums

C1 290440 60 69

Copyright © T E Moore 1992

First published 1992 by County Durham Books
in association with
Southgate Publishers Ltd
Glebe House, Church Street, Crediton, Devon EX17 2AF

Printed and Bound in Great Britain by Short Run Press Ltd, Exeter, Devon.

British Library Cataloguing in Publication Data.
A CIP catalogue record for this book is available from the British Library

ISBN: 1-897585-01-2

ACKNOWLEDGEMENTS

Illustrations:
British Steel Plc, front cover and p.87. North of England Open Air Museum, Beamish, pp.4, 36, 38, 39, 50, 58, 97. T. E. Moore, pp.31, 34, 40, 47, 89. Alan Reed, pp.102 twice, 103 twice.

In the preparation of this section, acknowledgement is given to the scores of people whom I have troubled at various times during the course of preparation and who seemed of such unending patience when attending to my enquiries.

In particular I would like to thank the Staff of Durham County Library Service for the help they have offered from time to time, and in particular Mr L. Storey of Consett Branch Library and the staff of Blackhill Trailer Library.

I would like to thank Mr Tommy Harris for his help.

I would also like to thank the staff of the following establishments:

Department of Environmental Health, Derwentside District Council, Tantobie.
Durham Reference Library, Reference section.
Durham County Record Office and Archives.
Gateshead Central Library Local History Section.
N.C.B. Coal House, Team Valley, Gateshead
Newcastle Central Library, Local History Section.
The Department of Paleography and Diplomatic, 5, The College, Durham University.

Acknowledgement is given of the courtesy shown and assistance in access offered by British Steel PLC, and of their Record Office in Commerce Way, Skippers Lane, Middlesborough. Acknowledgement is also given to Mr Jasper Scott of Blackhill in providing vivid and detailed descriptions of the blast furnace barrows of the day.

Particular thanks to Mr Dennis McKenna for the CIC coaster, the design of which appears on the front cover.

Tribute is paid to the following for their unreserved and ready acquiescence in the use of parts of their publications: Mr D. Harding, Head Teacher, Blackfine Comprehensive School, Consett, for kind permission to reproduce in part the Population Census Returns of the area of 1851; The Consett Lions for the use of The Consett Story; Mrs Margaret Crick of Blackhill and Mrs Maureen Allen of Bridgehill for their help and assistance.

READING LIST

Report on the Commissioners on the Truck Acts 1871, xxxvi; 1872 xxxv.
Whellans Directory 914.286 1896.
Report of Select Committee of the House of Commons on Application of Iron and Railway Structures, 1849.
British Parliamentary Papers (No. 1) 1839-49.
British Parliamentary Papers Mining Districts (No.2) sessions 1850-59.
Iron and Steel - Historic Industrial scenes   W. K. V. Gale
The British Iron and Steel industry   W. K. V. Gale
Eye Witness - The Industrial Revolution in the North-east, compiled by Edwin Miller of the Sunderland School of Education
Ironmaking before Bessemer   Barraclough
Industrial Archeology of North-east England   Frank Atkinson
Victoria History of the Counties of Great Britain vol. 2
The Economic History of the British Iron and Steel industry 1784-1879   Alan Birch
Industry and Technology in the Derwent Valley of Durham and Northumberland in the 18th century   M. W. Flinn
Iron and Coal   W.Fordyce
History of the North-eastern Railway   W. W. Tomlinson
The Railways of Consett and North-west Durham   G. Whittle
Rails between Tyne and Wear   C. R. Warne
Walking Northern Railways, vol 1; East   Charlie Emett
Monograph on Tinplate works in UK   E. H. Brooke
Chronology of Tinplate works   E. H. Brooke
Appendix to the Chronology of Tinplate of G.B.   E. H. Brooke
History of Staffordshire   W. Pitt
Towns in the Making   Burke
Durham University Journal 1971

A skyline to remember.

Cutting Boiler Plates.

CONTENTS

EPILOGUE *by Fred Robinson, University of Durham* **120**

APPENDICES

FOREWORD

A lot has happened to Consett in the last decade. Many people who grew up there and moved away would not recognize it today. Yet to know and understand Consett as it is today, to have a grasp of what binds the community together, despite the traumatic changes, we have to understand what and who made Consett.

Tommy Moore has given us a most detailed account of the early days of Consett and its surrounding communities. Consett, at one time the 'metropolis' of the iron and coal communities, has a great deal to teach us about the growth of the industrial north, and in this account the significance of the contributions of previous generations to the economic development of this country is crystal clear.

This account is much more than that, though, for it gives us a glimpse of the effect that the rush to capitalise on the new industrial processes had on people: those who had to labour long and hard to make a living, those who were brought to work and had difficulty finding homes, those who were involved in the riots of 1847.

I have thoroughly enjoyed reading this history of Consett, and have learned a great deal. The history of kings and queens is only very partial. Our history - of our families, our industry and our communities, is critical to our understanding of today, and the future. In an area which is so rich in history and of such great scenic beauty, the benefits and fulfilment of such research is much evident.

I hope that many other readers are able to enjoy Tommy Moore's 'Consett - A Town in the Making'.

HILARY ARMSTRONG M.P.

PROLOGUE

In 1992, as we look forward with anticipation and hope to the changing world order, it seems to me that this is a fitting time for this account of the history of Consett to appear. It serves as a timely reminder of the qualities, circumstances and history that has made Consett what it is.

Consett grew as a town with a purpose: a town built on enterprise, the taking of opportunities, use of its natural resources and the strength of character of its people.

With the closure of the steelworks in the early 1980s, we were once again thrown back onto these values. The future of our town depended on the creating of our own chances and seizing those opportunities that arose. For a decade we have steadily rebuilt our economy, encouraging new industry and taking care to protect our environment, our greatest asset.

The 1990s bring us to the dawning of a new era in the history of Consett and fittingly it is Berry Edge, the heart of the old town, which presents us with our greatest opportunity and our biggest challenge since the founding of Consett.

Working in partnership with the private sector and in consulation with the local community, we are embarking on the major task of redeveloping Berry Edge and bringing it back to its rightful place at the heart of our town. Like our predecessors we see Berry Edge as providing the key to our future prosperity and ensuring that the name of Consett is known throughout the world.

I commend this book to you as a symbol of the continuing growth and development of Consett - a testimony to a community's inbuilt resilience and capacity to develop. So long as people believe in themselves and have a vision for the future, communities will always overcome their temporary set-backs.

NEIL F JOHNSON
Chief Executive
Derwentside District Council

AUTHOR'S PREFACE

For many centuries the development of the county of Durham was influenced by the situation along the northern frontier with Scotland where warring factions kept the county in isolation. From the rest of England the county was subjected to successive destructive raids and wars over a long period.

The early settlements in the county were of Celtic origin and consisted of villages on the hilltops away from the woodlands and swamps of the lowlands. After the Romans came the Saxons who penetrated up the river estuaries. From the seventh century A.D. the Church began to take an important place in the county under Cuthbert, Patron Saint of Durham. The Normans were mainly responsible for the castles of Durham, Bishop Aukland and Barnard.

By the later Middle Ages the bishops had become so powerful that theirs was the only authority capable of maintaining order in this turbulent area. Durham therefore gradually emerged as a county palatinate with the bishops wielding considerable administrative and judicial power. It was not until the reign of Henry VIII that these powers were curtailed. Harrying from over the border finally ceased in the early part of the seventeenth century and the rural economy of the small villages of the county began to settle down.

As prosperity grew, several small-scale industries sprang up, mainly paper and linen mills along the rivers, and salt, glass and pottery near the coast. In west Durham, the mining of coal, iron and lead on a small scale attracted a considerable population and provided a market for the growing farming community. The present high and improved land in Weardale may have been cultivated to meet the needs of those engaged in mine workings.

The nineteenth century was a turning point in the history of the county, as two vital events took place on the eve of a great period of expansion. These were the enclosure of land and the industrial revolution.

The first drew people from the land and provided a large number of workers needed in the pits and the heavy industries. The rapid industrialization of the county was as a result of the iron and coal resources which could be easily extracted from the outcrops in the hilly areas of west Durham. The demand for coal for the south of England, the growth of shipbuilding, the construction of railways and the opening up of more distant markets, all gave impetus to changing the county's economy.

Until the late seventeenth century the valley of the river Derwent was a backwater which attracted few travellers. The only industrial activity of note in the valley was mining, the coalfields being reached by wooden wagonways. There are also indications that a limited amount of ironmaking had gone on in the area long before. Anglo-Saxon iron swords, axes and scythes were found in Hurbuck in 1870 near Smallhope Burn, and remains of early furnaces in the Lanchester area have been found.

During the seventeenth century Ambrose Crowley had established ironmaking works at Winlaton Mill and Swalwell, but lacked sufficient drive for it to continue. Because of this, ironmaking barely survived the eighteenth century, and had died out long before Bessemer and Mushet revolutionized the industry. The valley, however, remained an industrial centre of considerable potential. Its reawakening came in the late 1820s and early 1840s when the rediscovery of local ironstone led to the foundation of the Derwent Ironworks.

Between 1825 and 1850 ironworks were established in Winlaton, Consett, Tow Law and Witton Park, all based upon the local supply of raw materials. The Consett works, situated on the hilltop overlooking the valley, dominated the countryside for miles around. In just 140 years, Consett developed from a small village of a few cottages on a hillside dotted with grazing sheep, into a large and prosperous town and important community, whose products and name are remembered throughout the world wherever steel has been in demand.

It is therefore fitting to examine how those early settlements and industries grew into the large but somewhat isolated urban complex which owed its existence and prosperity to the vast modern integrated iron and steel works, whose site covered over 650 acres and which employed as many as 6,500 people.

Consett is the latest and arguably the greatest enterprise in the valley to fall under the hammer of industrial and economic progress. Situated in the upper Derwent valley, the town offers unspoilt views of woodland and upland as fine as any in the country, and reclamation of the area of the former Consett works for pleasure and recreation is now well under way. It will take many years to bring to fruition, but resurfacing, replanting and time will heal the wounds and scars on the land left by industrial progress and will return it to its former beauty.

It is ironic to think that, from those early years of hardship to the time of prosperity and greatness, and on to the closure and post-industrial era in which we live, that same piece of land which was significant in the birth of the early Consett works is the only industrial development remaining in use today. Coal had been mined in north-west Durham for many hundreds of years, while ironstone was only extracted for about 150 years to any great extent. It was the former which supplied the power and the latter which provided the impetus for the formation of the town of Consett.

This book is a small attempt to record the early years of Consett and of the people who made the town and industry possible.

TEM

CHAPTER 1
A History of the Area

*Consett prior to the 19th century; the history of roads in the area;
tythe maps; origins of the name Consett; population movements;
the growth of Consett*

CONSETT BEFORE THE NINETEENTH CENTURY

Historically, half (or moiety) of the Manor of Consett and the Park of
Conkesheved (Consett) had been held by Sir Thomas Gray, and descended to
Thomas Gray, Chivaler, in the fourteenth century. It then passed in turn to
Robert Nevill, Sir Thomas Gray and Sir Ralph Gray, who died in 1464; was
held by Thomas Gray until 1511, and then by Henry Anderson, merchant,
who died in 1572.

In 1579 Robert Blenkinsop acquired the estate from Anderson and died in
1588, leaving the estate to his son Charles. The Blenkinsop family still held
some of the estate in 1685.

The other half was held by William de Stobes. In 1422 it was vested in
settlement in Margaret, grand-daughter of William de Stobes, who had
married William Warde, and remained in the family until 1565. It then passed
by marriage to the Hall family of Birtley. In 1612 John Hall settled up his
estate and gave his eldest, although weakminded, son an annuity of £20.
When John Hall died the estate then went to his third son, Michael of
Durham. He was father to the celebrated John Hall of Grays Inn in the county
of Middlesex.

The Consett estate was purchased by Wilkinsons of Durham, who sold it to
Robert Curry of Bishopoak near Wolsingham, whose son disposed of it to
Jonathan Richardson, by whom it was conveyed to what later became the
Consett Iron Company.

FOOT PATHS AND ROADWAYS

Modern Consett, measuring 16 square miles, was established by the
amalgamation in 1937 of the small Urban Authorities of Consett, Benfieldside
and Leadgate plus the absorption of the parishes of Knitsley, Medomsley and
Ebchester belonging to Lanchester Rural District Council. Since then it has
been modified and reorganised to form a part of a greater local authority
structure which is Derwentside District Council.

Despite the passing of time, however, the road network of the area is essentially the same as it was for transport and communication in the seventeenth and eighteenth centuries. Many of these roads had no doubt originated as foot roads, following the safest, easiest and perhaps driest route between two or more centres of habitation.

At first no one, except the traveller himself, was responsible for the road, and that only so far as his own safety was concerned. Later, as common usage and custom demanded, the foot or roadway was then maintained for the common good by those living nearby. Other roads were specifically planned and laid down with the object of improving travel for the transport of the time.

The seventeenth century had seen the settling of rural farming communities in small villages throughout the county, whilst small industries sprang up to service the community. These were, quite understandably, related to coal, iron and even lead mining and were centred upon the ease of access of ore extraction.

However, as the population grew, transport became necessary not only for the social convenience of the populace, but also the commercial and industrial needs of the time. Power for industry existed mainly in the valleys where water was the main motive source, which then necessitated the transport of raw materials.

The roads as they existed in the late eighteenth century, including public highways of over 60 feet in breadth were:

	Present road designation
1) The Durham to Hexham road	A691, C10, A6309,B6310
2) Stanhope to Newcastle road	A692
3) Medomsley to Durham road	A691
4) Shotley Bridge to Durham road	B6310, A6309, A691
5) Shotley Bridge to Newcastle road	B6310, B6308
6) Shotley Bridge to Allensford road	A691, then Pemberton Road to Allensford
7) Medomsley to Stanhope road	B6308 then A692
8) Delfts (Delves) road	A692

1) THE DURHAM TO HEXHAM ROAD

This road led from the Stand-Against-All Farm (Burnhope) north westwards to Maiden Law and on to the Stanhope-to-Newcastle road (present day Jolly Drovers public house outside Leadgate). The Durham to Hexham route then continued south westward to join the Medomsley to Durham road and turned westward for 135 yards to join the Watling Street (at the present day Hat and Feather public house.) The route then joined the Watling Street, turning northward to meet the Shotley Bridge to Newcastle road (taking the present day Elm Park road) down to Shotley Bridge and on to Hexham).

2) THE STANHOPE TO NEWCASTLE ROAD

This was a turnpike road as is indicated on Ordnance Survey sheets of the time. The title of the turnpike trust is not clear, but it ran in part from Castleside to Consett, see also (7) below. It was described as 'being 60 feet in breadth, over and past certain moors or commons leading from a certain gate called Watergate near Cold Rowley aforesaid north east and east to Staniford Dam, whence the same highway continues through enclosures to Hounes and Coalburngate and thence continuing through the said moors or commons still eastward to Carrhouse Westgate and then on to Carrhouse Eastgate'. The route then crossed 'moorland and commonland to cross the highway called Watling Street and afterward crossing the Durham and Hexham road (Jolly Drovers public house) near Redwell Hill and thence east ward to Billingside, Pontop Dykes and Dipton'.

Coalburngate (unclassified) mentioned above was a private road at the time and was the existing minor road to Hownesgill viaduct and Knitsley just above the Stanifordham Dam public house at the Grove (see later Private Roads).

3) MEDOMSLEY TO DURHAM ROAD

'From Medomsley to continue south westwards to enter the Durham to Hexham road at or near the north west angle of the enclosure known as Bradley'.

4) SHOTLEY BRIDGE TO DURHAM ROAD

'From the south end of the village of Shotley Bridge and continue south westward along the Shotley Bridge to Allensford road, turning eastward to the end of the common quarry mentioned called Blackfine south common quarry' (present day Cutlers Hall and past Highgate), 'to the south east and then crossing the appointed Medomsley and Stanhope road' (Number One Roundabout). The route then 'turned south east to Carrhouse Eastgate, where it communicates with the Stanhope to Newcastle road' (bottom of Sherburn Terrace), 'following the Stanhope to Newcastle road to join the Medomsley to Durham road' (Jolly Drovers).

5) SHOTLEY BRIDGE TO NEWCASTLE ROAD

'From Snows Green to Medomsley and crossing the Durham and Hexham Road to Medomsley and thence to the Stanhope to Newcastle road', via Bradley, see (3) above.

6) SHOTLEY BRIDGE TO ALLENSFORD

'From the south end of the village of Shotley Bridge and continue south westward along the Shotley Bridge to Allensford road to John Johnsons allotment' (opposite Highgate public house), 'along Pemberton to Howden Burn, Consett Hedges to Pemberton House, at or near to the Allansford to Newcastle road' (present day Mutton Clog bank to the Grove). Pemberton

House stood a little below Mutton Clog bank and on the opposite side of the road, although it has long since disappeared.

7) MEDOMSLEY TO STANHOPE ROAD

This was a turnpike road as is indicated on Ordnance Survey sheets of the time. The title of the turnpike trust is not clear, but it ran in part from Castleside to Consett, see also (2) above. 'Leading south from the village to intersect the said Durham to Hexham road at Watling Street' (Hat and Feather public house) 'and across the Shotley Bridge to Durham road' (Number One) to communicate with the Stanhope to Newcastle road,' see (1) above, to meet at the cross roads in Consett town centre.

8) DELFTS (DELVES) ROAD

'...Leading from the said Stanhope to Newcastle road' (Consett town centre), 'southward to communicate with the Knitsley Mill road, Hurbuck road, West Road and the Knitsley Mill to Iveston road'.

In addition to the above, there were a number of lesser roads, 30 feet wide. These include

a) The Snows Green to Lanchester road, that is from Snows Green to Elm Park Terrace and up Elm Park Road (unclassified) and then to the Hat and Feather road to Lanchester via Leadgate.

b) The Snows Green to Shotley Bridge road, from Snows Green Burn to the village of Shotley Bridge.

c) Benfieldside Bank Road (unclassified) was the name used to describe the present day Church Bank from Shotley Bridge to Benfieldside Edge Road at the Quakers' Meeting house. In the days referred to, Benfieldside Edge Road was the name for present day Benfieldside Road prior to its extension past the Briary Down to Snows Green. The name was very descriptive as it indicated the extent of Benfieldside Parish, prior to the formation of the Township and Parish of Benfieldside in 1847. The extent of the Parish was further altered upon the formation of the Township and Parish of Conside and Knitsley in November 1862.

d) Barley Mill Road (unclassified; part known as Shotley Grove Road), from the south end of the village of Shotley Bridge, to run south and eastward to communicate with the aforesaid Shotley Bridge to Allensford Road at Pemberton.

'Each of the above roadways were laid at times hereafter from several breadths and that it should be lawful to all and for all persons whomsoever at all times hereafter to go, pass and repass on foot, horseback and with horse, coaches, carts and carriages and also to lead and drive all and all manner of cattle and other things in, through, over, and along the said respective public highways and roads at their free will and pleasure.'

Private Roads

In addition to the above it was also possible for a landowner to have a private way and passage to otherwise 'landlocked' parcels of land where no other access was otherwise available. As far as can be ascertained, two such roads were designated in the area.

Wilkinson's North Road (unclassified), which was also known as Black Lane by 1850. The north end became Cemetery Road in the 1860s, and the south end, Siemens Street in the 1880s, after the great steel maker of the time. Eventually this was later to become Laburnum Avenue in Blackhill. This was 20 feet wide,and was described as 'leading from the Shotley Bridge and Durham road' (at the present day Cricketers Arms public house) 'along the east side the the more improveable plot and parcel of the said Commons and Moors hereinafter alloted to Thomas Richardson, George Dixon and Esther Westgarth in respect of their copyhold established in the township of Benfieldside to Wilkinsons, for the use of the said heir Anthony Wilkinson. To pass and repass on horseback and horse carriages. But not to drive loose horses, cows, sheep or other cattle in, over, along the same way or passage'. Anthony Wilkinson owned over 80 acres of the land to the south of which was later sold to Jonathan Richardson about 1840 and which was the basis of the Derwent Iron Company.

Coalburngate and Hounes Road (see above) 'allowed access by the owner to his land. To pass and repass on horseback and horse carriages. But not to drive loose horses, cows, sheep or other cattle in, over, along the same way or passage.'

In about 1831, a main highway was driven along the direction of flow of the river Derwent from Shotley Bridge to Swalwell Bridge. This is now the main low road from Consett to Newcastle upon Tyne (A 694).

Foot Roads

There were many foot roads in the vicinity of Consett in the late eighteenth and nineteenth centuries.

1) Knitsley Mill to Crook Hall Road ran from Knitsley Mill northward and across Delfts road to Crook Hall, a distance of approximately 54 chains or 1086 metres.

2) Shotley Bridge to Consett foot road ran along the Shotley Bridge to Durham Road leading to Johnson's allotment (opposite Highgate), then leading south some distance before turning east to follow the foot road to Consett.

3) Shotley Bridge to Knitsley Mill road led from Shotley Bridge to Blackhill, along Wilkinsons North Road to the south end. A direct straight foot road was in use from there onto the crossroads of the main thoroughfare through

Consett, following the Delfts road to the Knitsley Mill road at the bottom of present day Delves Lane.

Other foot roads included

4) Staniford Dam to Cold Rowley foot road
5) Staniford Dam to Cragg House foot road
6) The Law and Medomsley foot road and
7) Snows Green and Bradley foot road

Each of the above foot roads were four feet wide 'delineated on the said Plan (Plan IV) annexed for use by one and all manner of persons whomsoever at all times hereafter to pass and repass on foot only in, through and along the said road'.

TURNPIKE TRUSTS (A691)

It is thought that there were two turnpike roads in the Consett area in the eighteenth century. One was the main Durham to Leadgate road via Witton Gilbert and Lanchester road. It was then to follow the much older routes to Number One, past Blackfine to Blackhill and Shotley Bridge and thence to Hexham.

Formation of TurnpikeTrusts

For more than a century the highways had been undergoing patchy and piecemeal improvement. This was encouraged by active Justices of the Peace and the Boards of Agriculture, anxious to give farmers better access to markets. All of these factors brought about the development of the Turnpike Trusts.

The great obstacle to improvement had lain in the fact that the upkeep of the roads was a parish responsibility. The roads were improved and repaired to the extent and by the methods that suited the people who lived there. The needs for long distance travel and transport were ignored, although horse riders and trains of pack horses could get around the holes and unsafe stretches of highways. The solution was the founding of Turnpike Trusts. These were heard of occasionally as early as the reign of Charles II but it was the difficulty of moving the army northward to meet the Jacobites in 1745 which caused the need for them to be generally recognized.

In 1773 a law was passed which made it easy to administer the trusts. Each trust consisted of local people who were willing to invest their money in improving a stretch of main road in their area. Having improved it and arranged for its upkeep they were empowered to recover their expenditure by a toll on every vehicle or beast driven along their road.

By an Act of Parliament and enclosure by the Church Commissioners the turnpike road between Durham and Hexham was authorised in 1810. The road leading from the city of Durham to Shotley Bridge passed through the parishes and parochial chapelries of St Margarets in Durham, Witton Gilbert, Lanchester and Medomsley.

It was recorded that:
All within the same county, passes through a barren and hilly and uneven part of the country and is otherwise inconvenient to the public; and it would be for the convenience of the inhabitants of the Parishes and places aforesaid and a public utility if the line of the present road from Durham to Shotley bridge were in many parts altered, and if the same were carried through Lanchester and if also the said road were straightened, widened and otherwise improved and kept in repair; but as the same cannot be effected by the laws in being for the amendment and preservation of highways.

There were about 144 trustees of the Durham to Shotley Bridge Turnpike Trust. They ensured the proper organisation, running and maintenance of the road. Fees were charged at tollgates placed at strategic places along the road, mainly where other roads led to or intersected the toll road.

Tollgates were erected for the purpose of collecting and receiving the tolls. The two tollgates which come immediately to mind were those called the 'High tollgate', which later became 'Highgate' in Blackhill, and the 'Low tollgate' at the bottom of Cutlers Hall road, which disappeared entirely when the toll charge system was abandoned.

With the formation of the ironmaking industry in the area, the rental charges laid upon certain tollgates can be seen as an indicator of a rising affluence in the area. The following advertisement indicates this:

DURHAM - SHOTLEY BRIDGE TURNPIKE
Notice is hereby given that the next meeting of the Trustees of the said Road appointed to be held at Smithenwaites at the sign of the Rose and Crown in Durham on Saturday 10th April 1841 at 11am, when the talks arising at the several undermentioned Tollgates erected on the said roads will be let by auction for one year to commence on the 18th May next.

The following are the annual rental charges for 1840 and 1841.

Toll gate	Rental charge (£) 1840	Rental charge (£) 1841
Witton Gilbert	140	136
Whitesmocks	130	122
Shotley Bridge	20	43
Fenhall	18	21

Decline and Fall of the Turnpike

By the late 1830s, when the coming of the railways brought the creation of new turnpikes to a halt, over 1100 trusts had been established covering 22 000 miles of road, including most of the main roads in the country. There still remained 105 000 miles of roads still in the care of the local parishes.

Inevitably, there was a rapid and calamitous fall in turnpike revenues as railways reached one region after another. The turnpike roads were ruined largely as a result of increasing railway passenger traffic, which accounted for nearly two thirds of railway gross receipts in 1845.

As for railway speeds, Stephenson had managed 15 m.p.h. on the Stockton and Darlington railway in 1825, 25 and 30 m.p.h. were known speeds in 1838, and by 1850 Great Western expresses were exceeding 50 m.p.h.

By 1890 there were only two turnpikes left in the country, and in 1895 the last toll levied on a public road was collected in Wales. From 1883 onwards the Government made grants to relieve taxpayers of part of the cost of maintaining dis-turnpiked roads.

There was no obligation for the Turnpike Trusts to spend any amount on the roads, which meant that little or nothing was being done in the way of improvements, although by 1838 an average of £51 a year was being spent per mile whilst parishes spent only £11 per year. Trusts usually only had jurisdiction over short stretches of road, therefore travellers over long routes had no control over the toll charges for their journeys.

Local people showed hostility to tolls as they too had to pay them. This problem led to an evasion of tolls and the hostility caused rioting and damage.

Many as the faults and difficulties of the trusts were, they were to give better methods of road maintenance and administration for many years. By the time of the Reform Bill, transport facilities were remarkably good in comparison with the those of 1750.

TYTHE MAPS

When churches were first built, the land around about supported them by paying a 'tythe' or tenth of the produce of the land to the church. The ancient Bishopric of the Palatinate of Durham kept a record of the various tythes which had been in operation since medieval times.

Tythes could be bought and sold, and lords or priests often sold them to other people. By the nineteenth century, tythes were being converted from goods and payment in kind, to money.

The following is an example of such a conversion to money value in respect of lands near Consett. Each of the occupiers of land mentioned are also recorded in detail in the census returns of 1851.

TYTHE MAP, CONSYDE AND KNITSLEY 1848

Name of Land owner	Occupier	Name of Lands	Quantity
Heirs of Geo.Baker	Anthony Shotton	Howens	200 acres
the same	Themselves	Howens Woodland	60 acres
Ralph Fenwick esq.	Thomas Marshall	Middle Gap	24 acres
Shaw	Thomas Marshall	Middles	24 acres
Thos.Robert} Swinburne}	Thomas Marshall William Bowey	Middles Head	70 acres
			378 acres

Made in Testimony 30th December 1842

Statement:-
Now I, J.Robert Rayson of Stockton on Tees in the County of Durham, having been duly appointed Valuer to apportion the total sum awarded to be paid by way of rent charge in Lieu of Tythes, among the several lands of the said Township of Conside with Knitsley. Do hereby apportion the rent charge as follows:-

Gross rent charge payable to the Tythe owner, in Lieu of Tythes for the township of Conside with Knitsley in the Parish of Lanchester.

£28. 18s. 4d.

The value of the tythe in imperial bushels and decimal parts of the imperial bushel of wheat, barley and oats was:

	Price per bushel £ - s - d	Bushels in decimal parts
Wheat	7 - 0¹/₄	27.45797
Barley	3 - 11¹/₂	48.70175
Oats	2 - 9	70.10101

The tythe found that the estimated quantity of land of the township came to 2617 acres. There was exempted land of 378 acres. This was made up from 252 acres arable land and 126 acres as meadow and pasture land, from the schedule of tytheable lands.

The apportionment of the actual tythe and rent payable was as follows:-

TYTHE MAP, CONSYDE AND KNITSLEY 1848

Acres, Roods, Perches	Name of Land owner	rent	Occupier	Name of Lands	Quantity
	Heirs of				
199-1-5	Geo.Baker	£21	Shotton	Howens	200 acres
56-1-4	the same		Themselves	Howens Woodland	60 acres
22-0-37	R. Fenwick	£2	Thos.Marshall	Middle Gap	24 acres
33-0-26	Shaw	£2-3s	" "	Middles	24 acres
69-2-27	Thos.Robert} Swinburne}	£3-5s-4d	Will. Bowey	Middles Head	70 acres
5-0-18	Stanhope and Tyne Railway	10s-0d			
	Total	£28-18s-4d			378 acres

The crops harvested on the land were oats, potatoes and turnips, wheat, seeds and wood. There was also clover and seed, and barley, with additional lands being made up of whins and woodland.

HISTORIC RECORDS OF THE NAME OF CONSETT

Consett was mentioned in the Boldon Book during the time of Bishop Pudsey (1153-1196) and in the later surveys by Bishop Hatfield.

The importance of these early works by the clergy of the time cannot be overstressed. The books contain the proceedings of the halmotes or courts held in the several manors of the County Palatinate of Durham. The word 'halmote' would seem to be a hall meeting, held in the hall of the bishop's manor house. The steward of the halmote would hold a court perhaps twice a year in the village or township which held the name of the manor. Anyone so summoned had to attend. The steward was assisted by a jury from each village, who were expected to advise the steward, possibly on local conditions or items of interest that could help him in his deliberations.

These manors, along with that of Lanchester (of which Consett was a part) covered a considerable proportion of the county. They amounted to the following:

Lanchester Manor included Benfieldside, Billingside, Butsfield, Satley, Broomshields, Kyo, Pontop, Roughside Broom-with-Flass, Roughside, Rowley and of course Lanchester.

Chester Manor covered those ares which included the present day Ryton, Whickham, Whitburn, Cleadon, Newton, Plawsworth, Boldon, Chester, Urpeth, Gateshead and Framwellgate.

Houghton Manor included Wearmouth, Ryhope, Burdon, Herrington, Newbottle, Murton, Wardon and Houghton.

Easington Manor included Sherburn, Cassop, Shotton, Shadforth and Easington.

Middleham Manor included Sedgefield, Cornforth and Middleham.

Stockton Manor included Carlton, Hartburn, Norton, Hardwick, Preston and Stockton.

Darlington Manor included Cockerton, Whessoe, Haughton, Blackwell and Bondgate in Darlington.

Sadberge Manor included Sadberge and Newbigging.

Auckland Manor included Rykenhall, Midridge, Heighington, Killerby, West Thickley, West Auckland, Redworth, Coundon Byers, Escomb, East Thickley, Newton Cap and Bondgate in Auckland.

Wolsingham Manor included Stanhope, Lynesack, Bishopley, Bedburn with Witton, Hamsterley and Wolsingham.

Bedlington Manor, formerly part of the County Palatinate of Durham, included East and West Sleekburn, Cambois and Bedlington.

Lanchester, like Wolsingham, was originally a forest vill, a small village in a forest clearing. As more and more forest land was cleared, more land was taken under cultivation. By 1183, these vills contained an unusually large number of tenants who, if they were not actually free, still formed no part of the villein community and paid rent to the Bishop instead of rendering services.

Under these circumstances with the abundance of empty land and a population more readily mobilised than the ordinary villein class, the rapid growth of new vills, which naturally retained a connection with the parent settlement, readily accounts for the formation of settlements on land further from the nucleus of the manor.

The Origins of the Name of Consett

Names of people and places inevitably become corrupted through centuries of use. It is sometimes quite easy to see the gradual change in the use of our language by looking at how names change.

A characteristic illustration of this is to be found in the name of the Palatinate capital, which is written Dunholm in the Saxon chronicle, A.D. 1072.

Other illustrations of this are the following items of word corruption circa 1570:

Cowardd	Cowherd
Beyst	Beast
Nygh'ors	Neighbours
Reange	Ringing
Wynnellyng	Winlaton

Perhaps in no instance in Durham has this tendency to corruption and contraction in language been more marked than in the name under consideration, Consett.

Some 700 years ago its name was Conkesheved, which may have originated from the Conke Burn (Cong Burn) which flows through Waldridge Fell and Chester-le-Street. However, this stream does not rise anywhere near the high plateau on which Consett stands. Another school of thought attributes the name to the fact that the area is in the shape of a rabbits head: Coneysheved or Coneyshead. Still another, and more likely explanation is the old English name 'Cuneca's headland'.

The original name and spelling of the town is not certain. The first mention of Conkesheved is in the Boldon Book, whose text was taken from a manuscript formerly kept in the Auditor's Office in Durham, but which is now in the Public Record Office in London.

There are two manuscripts, one from the Dean and Chapter of Durham, circa A.D. 1400 and the other in the Bodleian Library which is a transcript from the above. Both have the title as Cornesheved. These two however, are of a much later date than the Boldon Book.

In the Boldon Book 'in the year of Our Lords Incarnation' 1183, Arnold the Baker has Cornesheved (Consett) in exchange for Trillesdena (Tursdale) and renders 24 shillings.

It is interesting to note that a variation in spelling appears in Hatfield's Survey p. xv, where a knight who was present at the battle of Lewes (1264) between Henry III and the Earl of Leicester, had the name as Conkesheud. 'Con' is an Anglo-Saxon word for hill, and 'cheved' could be a corruption from 'chevage' or 'head' or 'chief', which was the sum of money paid to a lord or landowner for protection. Consheved could thus mean payment for the hilltop (remembering the elevation of the area.)

At some time in the past, the variable pronunciations of the name must have caused no little nuisance to the inhabitants as, in the Book of Rates for the County Palatine during the Commonwealth (1647), the name is given as 'Consett' alias 'Conside'. In several old documents the name of both Consett and Conside are used interchangeably. When the document is in Latin, then the name is usually Conside, whereas in English, the name is usually Consett.

The fact that Latin is a much older language and was in greater use at the time, presumably by the Palatinate Monks of Durham, suggests that Conside is the true name of the town. The fact that English was more commonly used, and the language was inevitably corrupted by the immigrant and indigenous population, caused the name to be read as Consett. Maps show Conside Hall on the site of present day Consett in 1625 and from the old documents and deeds it would appear that the name emerges from the somewhat cumbersome Conkesheved to Conshead, to Conside and finally to Consett.

Still other interpretations have been put forward, that the name Consett meant hill-top from the Anglo-Saxon. If, however, the Latin pronunciation of Conside is correct, then 'side' could mean a tract of territory of unknown or indeterminate extent, producing the interpretation of 'hill near territory of indeterminate extent'.

It has also been frequently if not recently called Berry Edge or Stobswoodhead. There are plausible explanations for this. The Anglo-Saxon for any open ground or wide expanse was 'beri'. Inhabitants of Consett know well that the town directly overlooks the open expanses of the Waskerley and the Muggleswick fells.

In Bishop Hatfield's Survey, a Thomas Gray and a William de Stobes jointly held the Manor of Conkesheved. There is evidence that the Derwent valley was very thickly wooded at this time, especially with oak. Stobswoodhead is therefore quite probably the adoption of the name of the joint holder of the manor.

Regardless of how the town got its name, it is more or less certain that the name Consett has been in use for upwards of 300 years.

NINETEENTH CENTURY POPULATION MOVEMENTS

The distinctive developments of the eighteenth-century towns and countryside were made possible by vigorous and solid progress in industry and trading. The upheaval in economic and social life that Arnold Toynbee named the 'Industrial Revolution' had its source in a mechanical revolution. An expanding home and overseas trade, stimulating production of a wide range of consumer goods and greater efficiency in methods of production, drew remarkable responses from inventive minds.

Newcomen's engine of 1712, for pumping water from mines, succeeded not only in increasing coal output, but was also used to drive factory machinery. Abraham Darby's new process (1709) of successfully smelting iron ore with coke, and Benjamin Huntsman's for steel (1740) expanded the iron and steel industry nationwide. James Watt's improved steam engine of 1783 could turn a wheel on a shaft and drive machinery.

These and other applications of machinery to manufacturing hastened the process of change from the cottage industry to the town factory and foreshadowed the concentrations of populations that characterized the industrial revolution. To the landowners and rich investors in this new technology, greater capital investment and the use of new machinery and methods meant greater efficiency. Experiments with crops and rotations and similar enterprises, could only be applied in large-scale production, i.e. large-scale farming units.

Enclosure, the only practical means of achieving larger units, had not been accepted under the Tudors and so had developed only slowly until the eighteenth century. After 1720, it made rapid progress in the south-east, west and north of England, with the encouragement of a long series of enclosures Acts of Parliament which were well disposed to landowners. Strips and smallholdings purchased from small farmers were regrouped into larger units and enclosed with hedges, so that sheep and cattle could be segregated for controlled breeding and given adequate pasture, while various crops could be grown in accordance with planned rotations in arable fields of approved sizes.

To the agricultural 'improvers', enclosure meant rational distribution of farming land to achieve greater productive capacity; to the central Government it was a means of meeting demands for food from an ever-increasing national population which was becoming more and more centred upon the towns; but to the small farmers and villagers it was an act of dispossession, bitterly resented and resisted, but finally imposed with devastating consequences for them.

The Enclosure Acts therefore increased the amount of land in the hands of the wealthy classes; the more enterprising small freeholders became large farmers, while the weaker and poorer men sank into the status of labourers, or took their chances in the towns.

The dislocation had not been universal, even where the enclosures were most widespread. In about 1830 roughly one fifth of English land was cultivated by its owners. On the other hand it was observed at the time that '19 out of 20' enclosure acts the poor were injured, 'in some cases grossly injured'. The compensation for a smallholding was meagre, perhaps a few pounds. The labouring families, in areas of recent and considerable enclosure, lost their customary privilege of stubbling on open fields or putting a beast on the common. The loss of fuel was also a hardship in winter.

Thus the dispossessed and homeless had little to choose between starving on the land or leaving it, to find means of living in the towns. With the new-found mechanical efficiencies in the latter, the likelihood of warmth and food must have been a powerful attraction, despite the long hours, low wages and poor housing that was offered.

This was the setting for the great leap forward which heralded the formation of the Derwent Iron Company, which laid the foundations of present-day Consett.

Of the early town, little is known. In larger towns, records were kept as the Government of the early years of the 1840s grappled with the problem of lamentable and insanitary conditions, with a whole succession of commissions and committees of enquiry. The toll of disease and the deplorable conditions in dwellings and workplaces coincided with an awakening public conscientiousness, with a will to improve the urban environment generally and living and working conditions for the 'lower' classes.

A significant step was the Municipal Reform Act of 1835. This transferred much of the power of local administration from the local monopolies of lawyers and professional people and landowners to the hands of local shopkeepers and tradesmen with a readier sympathy for schemes of improvement. This was followed by Shaftesbury's compassion for children exploited in mines, mills, chimneys and elsewhere, which brought the Factory Act to the statute book in 1844. Chadwick's work in ensuring more efficient water supply controls and drainage and sewerage led the way to combat waterborne diseases in the first Public Health Act in 1848. These three statutes were effected in the first nine years of the life of the Derwent Iron Company and the infant town of Consett.

John Vaughan, of Welsh upbringing and founder of Bolkow and Vaughan ironworks, was responsible for the introduction of Staffordshire ironmakers to Consett. Jenkins, the General manager of the Consett Iron Company from 1869 to 1894, was another prominent Welshman. As to the rank and file, experienced Staffordshire men of 'good character and steady habits' were recruited by being offered 'as inducements, good houses and gardens at a moderate rent, with other advantages'.

In Consett there was a similar report of workers being induced to come from all parts of England, Wales, Scotland and Ireland. Some needed no inducement, but came because they needed to work to live, to feed and clothe themselves and their families. At first this rapid integration of cultural mixes created social problems for which there were no adequate solutions, and for many years the Irish and indigenous populations of the town kept themselves segregated in all except work. This is dealt with in a later chapter of this book.

Benfieldside

Four or five centuries ago,the heights of Benfieldside would have been covered with forest, and the name would seem to be descriptive of the area. It first occurs in Bishop Hatfield's survey where the name is spelt Benefeldside. The Celtic 'ben' signifies an elevated place, while the suffix seems to have been derived from the Anglo-Saxon 'feld', a forest clearing. Thus the name suggests 'a hill at the side of a forest clearing'.

Page 26. **District outline of Benfieldside Township 1847.**

Page 27. **District outline of Consett 1862.**

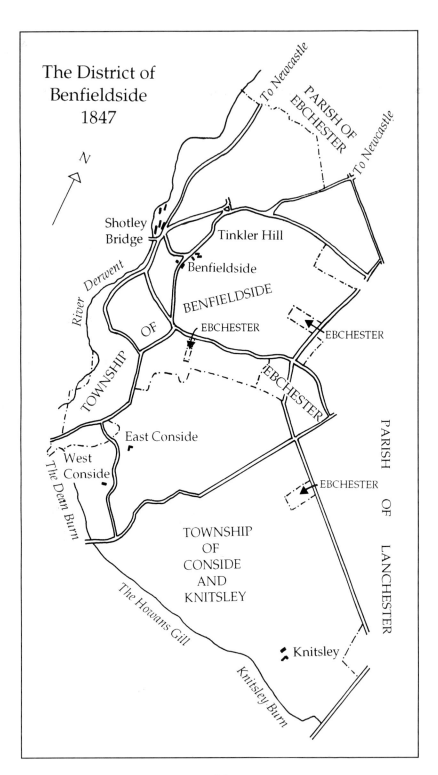

The District of
Benfieldside
1847

N

PARISH OF
EBCHESTER

To Newcastle

To Newcastle

To Newcastle

Shotley
Bridge

Tinkler Hill

River Derwent

Benfieldside

BENFIELDSIDE

EBCHESTER

EBCHESTER

TOWNSHIP

OF

EBCHESTER

East Conside

West
Conside

The Dean Burn

EBCHESTER

PARISH OF LANCHESTER

TOWNSHIP
OF
CONSIDE
AND
KNITSLEY

The Howans Gill

Knitsley

Knitsley Burn

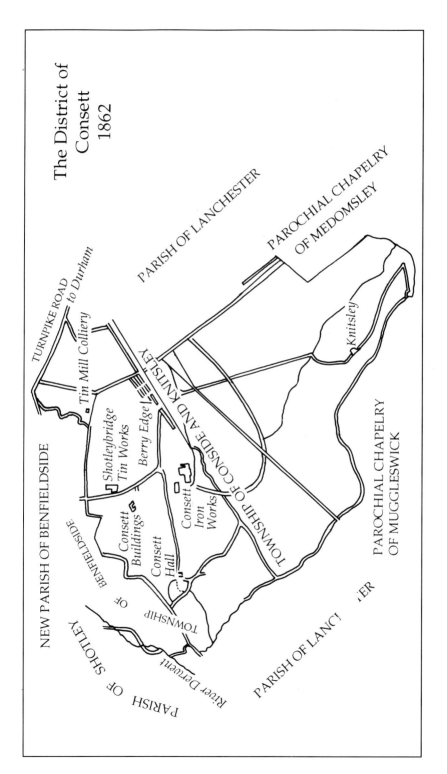

The District of Consett 1862

PARISH OF LANCHESTER

PAROCHIAL CHAPELRY OF MEDOMSLEY

TURNPIKE ROAD to Durham

Tin Mill Colliery

Knitsley

TOWNSHIP OF CONSIDE AND KNITSLEY

Berry Edge

Shotleybridge Tin Works

NEW PARISH OF BENFIELDSIDE

OF BENFIELDSIDE

Consett Buildings

Consett Hall

Consett Iron Works

PAROCHIAL CHAPELRY OF MUGGLESWICK

PARISH OF LANCI ...ER

TOWNSHIP OF

PARISH OF SHOTLEY

River Derwent

PARISH OF LANCI ...ER

The population figures of Benfieldside exploded in the early and mid 1800s. This can be seen in the following:

Year	Population
1811	275
1821	341
1831	534
1841	1074
1851	2475
1861	4026
1871	4434
1882	5857

In 1831 there were 81 inhabited houses and by 1882 there were 1055 houses. By the 1840s the need to form Benfieldside into a separate township was apparent. By 10 August 1847 an Order In Council constituting a separate district out of the Chapelries of Ebchester and Medomsley was made, to be called 'The District of Benfieldside'. This was done by an Act 'to make better provision for the spiritual care of populous Parishes'.

Benfieldside was to consist of 'all that part of the Chapelry of Medomsley in the Parish of Lanchester in the County and the Diocese of Durham, comprised within the Township of Benfieldside and such portion of the Township of Conside and Knitsley, in the same Chapelry as is situated in the northern side of the Dean Burn, the Howans Gill and Knitsley Burn; and also all of those small detached portions of the Parochial Chapelry and Township of Ebchester in the same Parish situated to the south of the high road from Shotley Bridge to Newcastle, by Tinkler Hill (Elm Park)'.

In 1866 the Benfieldside Local Board was formed. Because of the nature of the land surrounding, part of it was under the jurisdiction of the Lanchester Highway Board at the time. A considerable part of Blackhill at that time was under the control of the Consett Sanitary Board. As there was a need for adequate drainage, the Blackhill proportion of the Consett Sanitary Board was connected to the Benfieldside main sewer for which the Consett Sanitary Board paid Benfieldside a certain sum each year.

Under the provisions of the Local Government Act of 1894, the Benfieldside Urban District Council of twelve members was formed, which took the place of the former Local Board. Benfieldside was said to include Shotley Bridge, Blackhill and the off-shoots of Snows Green, Benfieldside, Cutlers Hall, Shotley Grove and Bridgehill and was very scattered until it was amalgamated with Consett and district to form the Consett Urban District Council in 1937.

GROWTH OF CONSETT TOWN

Consett was once described as the metropolis of the ironmaking and coalmining communities in the north-west of the County of Durham. Long before the Derwent Iron Company had commenced operations and ironstone had been mined for some years, accommodation for the workmen had been necessary near the surface or mine workings. These centred upon the road routes which had formed in the area.

In a very short time, what amounted to a prospectors' camp was set up high up on the east bank of the Derwent Valley, at the time a wild rural district of the county. This was where the original nucleus of the town was laid, and where it still is today. The crossroads of the two main through roads which run through the town, roughly north-south and east-west, still exist, the first from Delves Lane to Medomsley and the second from Castleside to Leadgate.

This then, was the most convenient area for the building of houses for the immigrant workers arriving almost every day into the settlement. Next came the shops, the hotels, churches and theatres, thrown up as and when need required to satisfy the demand that arose from that ever- rising tide of population, which had increased 14-fold in just ten years. As land became more scarce, half-forgotten wagonways that had ceased to function, were brought back into use. These roads were later to be adopted and named after various Victorian gentry and aristocrats as, for example, John Street, Raglan Street and Albert Road.

The undisciplined pressures for shelter gave a great impetus to an unparallelled programme of private building. The effect of this was that hovels, houses, schools and business premises alike were sited as the construction and the needs of the moment dictated without much, if any, thought for the future. This resulted in a confused system of streets and an illogical mixture of housing and business premises.

This illogicality was added to by the intermingling of each with cul-de-sacs, streets ending abruptly at quarry edges and at quarry faces, or with streets of undesirable gradients, steepness and inadequate width. While growth took place in those early years, little or no pattern was followed until after the formation of the township on 1 November 1862. Only after that date was development controlled by a code of by-laws which made certain hygienic provisions and demanded streets to be of certain minimum widths. These by-laws, being limited in scope, were only able to control the line of streets for traffic purposes and not for social requirements. However, the very fact of the uncontrolled beginnings of the town and of the appearance of lack of orderliness has retrospectively given the town that sense of character and quality which was at first thought lacking.

To explain in minute detail the social, political and economic mores of a newly formed industrial town of Victorian England would be quite a task. What follows is but a brief overview of events during the early years of the town. My only wish in setting this down is to ensure that the tiny piece of history which was the Consett of its day will not be forgotten.

CHAPTER 2
The Coming of the Railway

The first railways; complexities of ownership; railways associated
with the Consett works; gradual closure

RAILWAYS OF THE CONSETT AREA

As the birthplace of the railways, County Durham is haunted by the ghosts of its former greatness, as the Tanfield or Causey Arch will testify. The greatness of the area could only have been achieved by this mode of transport, for out of the railways came the growth in coal production, the collieries and the iron and steel industry of north-west Durham.

Most of the region between the Tyne and Wear lies on the Great Durham coalfield which is exposed to the west and concealed under layers of magnesium limestone in the east. West of the coalfield lies the open moorland of north-west Durham, composed mainly of millstone grit and carboniferous limestone. The exposed coalfield in the centre of the region was the first area to have railways because of the vital need to remove the accessible coal to the manageable sections of the two rivers. The second area to be developed was the moorland area to the west of Consett, for this contained valuable deposits of limestone and lead.

Although primitive wooden railways (or wagonways) had been laid down to the Tyne and west of Gateshead and to the Wear around Fatfield in the early seventeenth century, as technology improved with the introduction of inclined planes, static steam winding engines, iron rails and finally steam locomotives, the wagonway network was extended further inland to the watershed between the two rivers, and westwards to include both sides of the Derwent valley.

It was in County Durham that, in 1825, the world's first passenger train, named *Locomotion*, made its historic journey from Shildon to Darlington and Stockton. Thus was born a mode of transport which was to revolutionize travel worldwide. Within a decade of the opening of the Stockton and Darlington Railway, the advantages of building railways and carrying goods and passengers had been proved.

The speed with which public steam-operated railways came into operation produced a conflicting network of routes composed of coal-exporting lines running roughly west to east with essential communicating lines between the major centres of population of Teesside, Durham city and Tyneside, Sunderland and South Shields. Added to this conflict were the effects of major landowners who could disrupt or even thwart railway routes; rivalry

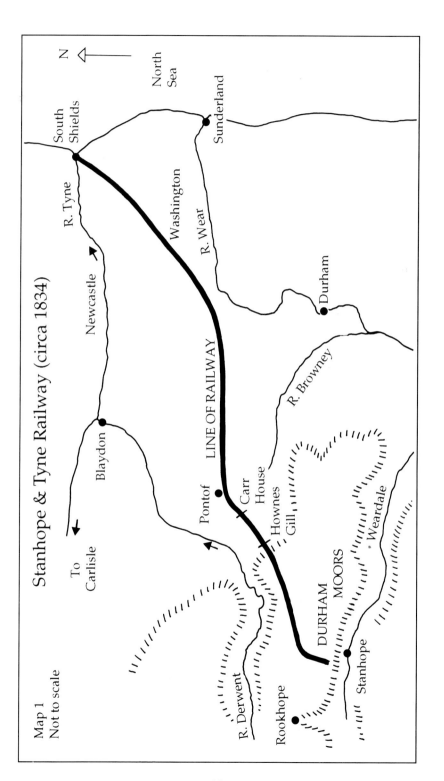

Map 1
Not to scale

Stanhope & Tyne Railway (circa 1834)

N

North Sea

South Shields

Sunderland

R. Tyne

Washington

R. Wear

Newcastle

Durham

To Carlisle

Blaydon

LINE OF RAILWAY

R. Browney

Pontof

Carr House

Hownes Gill

Weardale

R. Derwent

Rookhope

DURHAM MOORS

Stanhope

between the Tees, Tyne and Wear for coal shipment contracts, and even rivalry between the upper and lower sections of individual rivers. Rivalry between the different railway companies of the day added even more to the complexities of forming the railway network of the Durham region. The railway was of great value to Consett. Its presence and continued use kept Consett, and many other similar places, alive. I have examined only a tiny part of the Durham network of railways, to follow the development of the railway system of the Consett area, from before the town came into being, to the fully grown iron and coal industry as it existed, with internal networks of railways and rolling stock, to the external railway systems which were so vital for the industry's survival for the import and export of its raw materials and finished products throughout the world. No doubt many may feel as I do, that the town's railways were as much a part of its industry and lifeblood as was the iron and steel industry itself.

Stanhope and Tyne Railway

Medomsley was one of those numerous agricultural villages caught up in the activity of coal mining in the 1830s. Stanhope in Weardale was a centre for the extraction of limestone. In 1831 Messrs Harrison and Barnard, limestone quarry owners, planned to open a large limestone works in Stanhope. About the same time, Pontop colliery, which had lain idle for five years, and a landsale pit at Medomsley were advertised to be let. The lease was taken up in 1833 by the Stanhope and Tyne Railway Company, which was desperately trying to make its expensive new railway pay for itself, by acquiring pits to keep it supplied with freight.

The company took it over on the advice of its consultant, Mr Buddle. The principal seam of the Pontop pit was said to be 'of great extent and of great valuable deposits, being 6 feet 7 inches at the Hutton seam level'. The intention was to carry the coal and lime from Medomsley, via the river Derwent, probably down the old Pontop Wagonway (opened in about 1739), which ran from Pontop to Derwenthaugh via Rowlands Gill. It was then decided to build the railway from Stanhope to some point on the Tyne.

Stanhope was connected by rail to Medomsley colliery, over the high bleak moors of Waskerley, using rope haulage and inclined planes. It was a very difficult route, with a rise of over 1400 feet above sea level. Soon the plans were enlarged into considerations for a line from Stanhope to Tanfield Moor, where the Tanfield wagonway would continue the route to the Tyne at Dunston. It was soon acknowledged that this line, if constructed to Dunston, would link Stanhope with the wrong part of the Tyne and that the services of the keelmen would be required. The question was asked 'why not go to the deep water port of South Shields and so save shipment costs down the river Tyne?' If there was a rail link between Stanhope and South Shields then limestone could be exported as well as coal from Medomsley, through the outport of the mouth of the Tyne.

The logic of the argument was accepted by the promoters, despite the inherent severe civil engineering difficulties in the scheme. An ambitious prospectus had been prepared in 1832 with Mr T. E. Harrison appointed as residential engineer. For good measure and for prestige, Robert Stephenson was persuaded to become the consulting engineer.

There was no act of Incorporation from Parliament, as the old wagonway wayleave system was to be used. The land on which the Stanhope and Tyne railway was built was leased from the Dean and Chapter of Durham Cathedral at rents which, in places, were to prove so exorbitant that they were to lead to the railway's eventual collapse some years later.

In May 1833 work began on the lower section from Stanley down to South Shields. The old Pelton Fell wagonway was used in part, and a site for the quay at South Shields was selected and a deed of settlement for wayleaves was signed on 3 February 1834. In November 1833 work was completed on bridges and embankments in South Shields, and on 1 May 1834 the first locomotive, built by Robert Stephenson, was placed on the track at South Shields.

On 15 May 1834, the $15^1/_4$ mile upper section between Stanhope and Annfield was opened. Unfortunately the occasion was marred by the death of three people resulting from a snapped haulage rope that caused four wagons to run out of control on the Weatherhill incline above Stanhope.

Finally on 19 September 1834 the lower section from Annfield to South Shields was opened. At about the date set for the opening of the railway, an engine arrived from the Medomsley and Pontop pits with a hundred wagons of coal which was loaded into the ship *Sally* at South Shields. The locomotive that shunted this historic load was built by a joiner and blacksmith at Annfield Plain. The boiler of this engine burst in 1837, killing the driver and the fireman.

The complex route had a total length of over 37 miles and included all known forms of power of the day. These were utilised in the following proportions (see map 2): by horse haulage: $14^1/_2$ miles; by nine stationary steam engines: 11 miles; by locomotive haulage: $9^1/_4$ miles; and by self-acting inclines: 3 miles.

Despite the early enthusiasm, the Stanhope and Tyne was found to have been a rash venture. It had an almost impossible route based on inaccurate and over-optimistic assumptions about potential trade (see map 1). A very serious error had been made in establishing the entire line on the old wayleave system, rather than seeking an Act of Incorporation. As a result many of the landowners charged sky-high rents on a 21-year lease, and there was nothing the Stanhope and Tyne could do about it. In order to raise all the capital, very high interest rates needed to be charged. Earnings were well below expectation and a mortal blow came in mid-1839 when the Stanhope limeworks went bankrupt and were closed down. The result was an entire shutdown of the line from Stanhope to Medomsley.

Another serious blow came in November 1839 when the Tanfield Moor

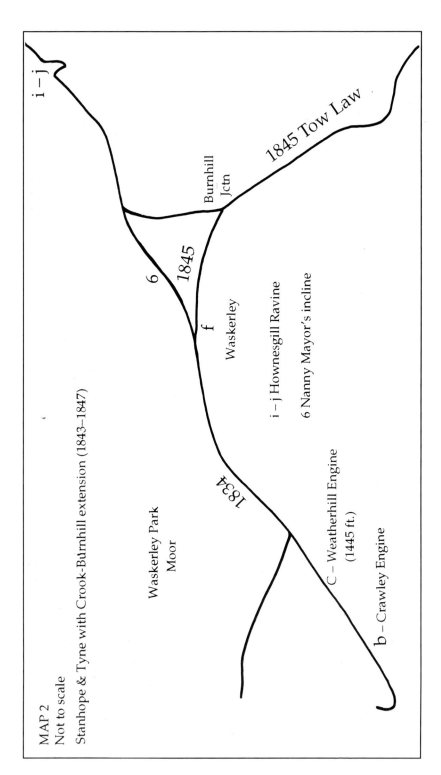

MAP 2
Not to scale
Stanhope & Tyne with Crook-Burnhill extension (1843–1847)

Waskerley Park
Moor

i – j

1845 Tow Law

Burnhill
Jctn

6

1845

f

Waskerley

i – j Hownesgill Ravine

6 Nanny Mayor's incline

1834

C – Weatherhill Engine
(1445 ft.)

b – Crawley Engine

colliery stopped using the Stanhope and Tyne railway and resumed using the Tanfield branch line to the Tyne once again. The combined effect of these two catastrophes, plus the untenable wayleave charges was too much, and in December 1839 the Stanhope and Tyne railway found that it could not meet its liabilities.

Worse was to follow for the owners. Because it had not been incorporated by an Act of Parliament, individual shareholders had unlimited liabilties in respect of their interests in the company. Robert Stephenson had agreed to accept shares in lieu of cash as his consultancy fees, so he was in a desperate situation which looked like spelling ruin for him. In an attempt to escape the financial horrors of the situation, Stephenson himself chaired a meeting on 29 December 1840 to launch a new and properly incorporated company to absorb the moribund Stanhope and Tyne railway. This new company was to be called the Pontop and South Shields Railway.

The fact that the railway almost passed through Consett and near the Derwent Iron Company had been a decisive factor in the ironworks' establishment. Now it needed the western section of the Stanhope and Tyne Railway to keep itself functioning. The Derwent Iron Company used the line to obtain coal from Medomsley and limestone as flux from Stanhope. It therefore decided to purchase and use the western section of the railway, from Stanhope to Medomsley. This section then became known as the Derwent Railway and was in use by the Derwent Iron Company for some years before finally passing to the North Eastern Railway in 1863.

A complex story follows the collapse of the Stanhope and Tyne Railway, and the consequent need of the newly founded ironworks at Consett to safeguard its supply of raw materials. The ironworks realized that its ironstone deposits were not limitless, and that it would be necessary to import those materials. It made an excellent offer to the Stockton and Darlington Railway in which it was prepared to lease it the former Stanhope and Tyne Railway section which it owned, and to sponsor the building of a line from Crook to Burnhill, to be carried out by the Stockton and Darlington Railway. As the work would be financed by the ironworks no Act of Incorporation would be required.

The rugged relief made this a hard task, but the offer was a good one and work on the new Crook to Burnhill line, which was immediately called the Weardale Extension Railway, began in 1844. To rise up out of Crook, a $1^3/_4$ mile inclined plane of 1 in 13 was needed, called the Sunniside incline. The line passed through Tow Law to join the Derwent Railway at Waskerley. Here, at this bleak moorland junction, the headquarters and maintenance base of this line was established. It opened for goods in May 1845 and for passengers four months later. The Derwent Iron Company promptly leased the former Stanhope to Medomsley section to the Stockton and Darlington Railway as agreed and this was then renamed the Wear and Derwent Railway. This arrangement paved the way for close co-operation between the Stockton and Darlington Railway and the Derwent Iron Company for many years to come.

Following the scheme, both of these sections, from Stanhope to Medomsley and from Crook to Burnhill unofficially became known by the same name. Passenger services were started from Crook to Waskerley Park and thence to Crawleyside Bank above Stanhope, and also to Rowley.

In retrospect, the arrangement can be seen as being a very far-sighted and wise move on behalf of the owners of the Derwent Iron Company, as it gained access to the south of the county, for fresh supplies of iron ore, and access to the river Wear as an outport for its products. It may have considered that, were too much reliance to be given to the Tyne as an outport, this might have led to problems in the future.

An interesting feature still visible today from above Healeyfield Bridge on the Waskerley way, is the 'Nanny Mayor's incline' between Waskerley and Whitehall and Rowley (see map 2). Today, faint parallel lines of what remains of a self-acting incline are still visible reaching uphill, at an angle away from the direction of the Waskerley Way, adding to the beautiful moorland vistas, made more dramatic by the ever-changing weather and seasons, toward Waskerley. Nanny Mayor's incline was almost $2/3$ of a mile long with gradients of between 1 in 10 and 1 in 134 and was capable of dealing with eight wagons each way. The name came from a Mrs Nanny Mayor who kept a lineside alehouse on this stretch of the railway.

In those days, travellers disembarked at the bottom of the incline to be transported by horse-drawn dandy carts along it to the next obstacle, Hownesgill ravine. As can be imagined, passenger services direct to Consett were not to start for a number of years because of the Hownesgill ravine.

Nanny Mayor's incline overlooking Consett in the distance.

Hownesgill Ravine

For the builders of the Stanhope and Tyne railway, Hownesgill ravine presented a major obstacle. It was a glacial spillway forming a gorge which was 150 feet deep and 800 feet wide, aligned across the path of the intended railway. It would have been difficult to make a detour round the gorge. A bridge was the obvious solution but because of the poor state of the Stanhope and Tyne Railway's finances, the company was not able to build a viaduct across the precipitous, dry gorge. The time factor had to be considered, to ensure that the railway opened on time. It seemed as though the only solution was to erect inclined planes down each side of the gorge.

These inclined planes have been described as 'one of the railway's most original features' at the time. Mounted on the floor of the gorge was a 35 hp stationary steam engine manufactured by Robert Stephenson, which worked both the precipitous slopes. The wagons were lowered down the slopes in cradles, one on each incline, the wagons being held horizontally. Turntables at the top of the incline allowed the wagons to be turned to right angles of the lines themselves. The cliff cradle arrangement in which wagons were lowered one at a time on a gradient of about 1 in $2^1/_2$. At the bottom turntables enabled the wagons to be pushed off the cradle for a few yards to be repositioned in the opposite ascending cradle to be hauled up a gradient of some 1 in 3, then shunted off to wait the assembly of other trucks in the train. Later the system used funicular railways on each side hauled three trucks up at a time, but it was little better than the original system.

On average only twelve wagons an hour could be taken over the gorge, and it soon became a bottleneck. As a result serious delays were experienced for a number of years.

Hownesgill Viaduct

At about the time that the Crook-Burnhill line was opened in 1844, it was recommended that a tension iron viaduct upon four stone pillars of strong rubble, containing the whole space in five spans of 53 yards, should be built.

A structure of this kind could not be built for less than £10,000. It was not until 1856 that the recommendation was taken up by the Stockton and Darlington Railway again, which by then had suffered severely as a result of the bottleneck. The design was by William Boucher and approved by the railway in December of that year. It was mainly of firebrick and had twelve semi-circular arches supported by pillars of light proportions carrying the railways at a height of 150 feet above the ground.

The cost came to £14,000 and the contractor, Mr John Anderson, used about $2^1/_2$ million firebricks. The structure took some seventeen months to complete and was opened on 1 July 1858. The viaduct had stone abutments and iron railings along each parapet and was suitable only for a single line of traffic. The old inclines were dismantled and the station nearby was closed.

Hownesgill Viaduct c.1890.

The 150-foot-high Hownesgill viaduct is ten feet higher than the High Level Bridge which spans the river Tyne, and can still be seen from miles around.

The Wear Valley Railway

In 1847 the Wear and Derwent Railway, together with the Bishop Auckland and Weardale Railway, became legally known as the Wear Valley railway (see map 3). It was leased to the Stockton and Darlington Railway for 999 years and was fully incorporated into the Stockton and Darlington Railway in July 1858. The Wear Valley Railway had been incorporated by Act in July 1845 but had no effects until July 1847.

The foregoing were then the main arterial rail-links with which the Derwent Iron Company (1841-58), the Derwent & Consett Iron Company (1858-64) and the Consett Iron Company (1864-1967) forged its transportation and communication links with the outside world. In later years many other rail links were to be laid to assist the growing industrial town of Consett. The railway facilities did not, however, fully satisfy the industry's needs, and efforts were continually being made to improve the network, especially in the areas of south-east Durham and north Yorkshire.

As the first step in a scheme of amalgamation of the Durham railway system, the Stockton and Darlington Railway company bought the Stanhope-Carrhouse line from the Derwent Company in 1846, and by 1847 had almost brought financial disaster on its head by increasing its network of rail links in west Durham. The railway company was only saved by the opening of the Cleveland ore deposits in which the Derwent Iron Company was interested.

WEAR & DERWENT
JUNCTION RAILWAY.

On the 1st of APRIL, 1846,

Trains for the Conveyance of Passengers will commence running every Day (Sundays excepted) from COLD ROWLEY and CRAWLEY near Stanhope, to CROOK, in connection with Trains to and from Darlington, Stockton, York, &c.

TRAINS LEAVE	1st Trip. A.M.	2nd Trip. P.M.		TRAINS LEAVE	1st Trip. A.M.	2nd Trip. P.M.
Cold Rowley at	**6·0**	**4·0**		Crook - - at	**8·50**	**5·30**
Crawley near Stanhope	**6·0**			Waskerley Park	**9·50**	**6·30**
Waskerley Park	**6.30**	**4·30**		ARRIVE AT		
				Cold Rowley -	**10·20**	**7·0**
Crook	**7·30**	**5·30**		Crawley, for Stanhope		**7·0**

J. READMAN, PRINTER DARLINGTON.

Railway Timetable 1846.

Evidence of the Stockton and Darlington holdings remains today on the stretch of the Waskerley Way Country Park between Waskerley and Stanhope where it is still possible to see carved stone boundary posts marked simply 'S & D' standing as they were placed when they took the line over from the ironworks.

The 54-mile haul from Cleveland and north Yorkshire to Consett became an important source of income to the railway and remained so for a considerable time to follow.

Extensive Internal Railway Lines *(see map 3)*

The Derwent Iron Company also owned and operated two rail branches of its own, namely the Medomsley and South Medomsley branches.

MEDOMSLEY BRANCH

A mile-long branch of the North Eastern Railway (NER) Pontop and Shields line went from the Bradley ironworks, half a mile west of Leadgate station, to Medomsley colliery. In 1856 the Derwent pit was sunk one mile north east of Medomsley colliery. The Hunter pit just south of the Derwent pit, was opened in 1889. The Consett Iron Company owned both of these pits and worked the one mile line to the NER Medomsley branch. In 1924 the London and North Eastern Railway (LNER) sold the whole Medomsley branch to the Consett Iron Company, which operated it until the takeover by the National Coal Board in 1947.

SOUTH MEDOMSLEY BRANCH

A colliery was opened in 1861 and initially was called the Pontop Hall colliery. It was served by a one-mile branch from the NER Pontop and Shields line and was operated by the NER. The ironworks continued to work the traffic on this branch between 1862 and 1884.

In the early years there were also subsidiary lines to other ironworks, at the Bradley ironworks, Crookhall ironworks of 1845 and the Shotley Bridge Tin and Ironworks, which manufactured tinplate until 1863 when it changed ownership to become the Shotley Bridge Iron Company. These were all at one time or another absorbed into the larger concern which was to become the Consett Iron Company

In addition to many of the external lines developed by the ironworks in the Consett area, there were necessary lines of supply within the ironworks, to coke ovens and blast furnaces and other ancillary plant and also to the collieries. Map 3 gives a diagramatic layout of the railway system as it developed in later years.

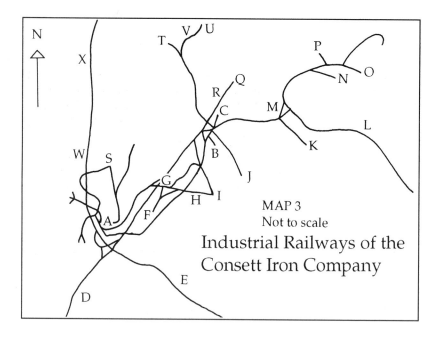

MAP 3
Not to scale
Industrial Railways of the Consett Iron Company

THE LEGEND TO MAP THREE

A)   Consett Ironworks
B)   Crookhall Ironworks
C)   Bradley Ironworks
D)   Derwent Railway (1842-45), now the Waskerley Way

E)   Lanchester Branch, now the Lanchester valley walkway
F)   Templetown Locomotive sheds
G)   Latterday Saints pit (Victory pit)
H)   West Ellimore pit
I)   Crookhall colliery
J)   Iveston colliery
K)   Brooms drift
L)   Pontop & Shields branch line
M)   Eden colliery
N)   Pontop
O)   Pontop Hall
P)   Mary pit
Q)   Billingside drift
R)   Bradley colliery
S)   Tin Mill colliery (at the top of Consett park)
T)   Medomsley colliery
U)   Derwent colliery
V)   Hunter pit
W)   Blackhill station
X)   Blackhill & Scotswood line (the Derwent walk) at Swalwell.

In 1891 the mines railway and staithes at Derwenthaugh belonging to the Chopwell and Garesfield Railway were all sold to the Consett Iron Company. Under its ownership, the line was rebuilt and further extended to Chopwell. The Derwenthaugh staithes were enlarged in 1913 to accomodate the extra traffic generated by this successful line. Today even the section from Derwenthaugh staithes to the Derwenthaugh cokeworks is closed and nearing complete demolition. This ends a long history of railway and wagonways along this stretch, dating back as long as 1739 on the south Tyneside wagonway.

OTHER RAILWAY SCHEMES WITH WHICH THE CONSETT STEELWORKS WAS ASSOCIATED

1) Blaydon and Consett Branch Line (1864-1963)

The alternative scheme offered by the NER in 6 (below) was the Blaydon and Consett branch line, alternatively known as the Derwent Valley Line. The first proposals for the Derwent valley were made by the NER when they were hurriedly prepared in 1859 as the Blaydon to Conside Branch in order to oppose the Newcastle and Derwent Valley Railway Proposals (see 5 below).
    This challenge was successfully repelled in 1860, but a second was to follow (see 4 below) which was very nearly successful. The NER therefore submitted

a third bill to Parliament in November 1861 and this was granted an Act on 30 June 1862. The success of this line was dependent upon the prosperity of the ironworks, which was undergoing a very severe financial crisis in 1862. In May 1864 however, the Consett Iron Company was formed, and no doubt added to the impetus of building the line.

The railway line was $10^{3}/_{4}$ miles long and followed the Derwent valley from the Scotswood junction to Blackhill, with stations at Swalwell, Rowlands Gill, Lintz Green, High Westwood, Ebchester and Shotley Bridge (this last was originally called Snows Green station). The line was a steep pull up all the way from the Tyne, with an almost uninterrupted 1 in 66 incline for the last $7^{1}/_{2}$ miles. There were notable viaducts at Swalwell, Lockhaugh, Rowlands Gill, Lintz Green and Hamsterley Mill. The track was single laid, except between Rowlands Gill and Lintz Green.

The Blaydon and Conside (later Blaydon and Consett) branch of the LNER railway was opened for freight on 18 June 1867 and to passengers on 2 December 1867, linking Blackhill to Tyneside along the valley of the Derwent. Travellers to Consett had to complete the journey by horse-drawn carriage from Blackhill to Consett. Blackhill station,which was originally Benfieldside Railway Sidings, after the parish in which it stood, was estimated to have cost £9500. Blackhill station was first called Benfieldside in 1867, then Consett in 1882, then Consett and Blackhill 1885, and then finally Blackhill 1896.

The first services for passengers comprised three trains each way per day and the average journey time was about 51 minutes, with extra services being laid on for weekends. Passenger traffic increased enormously in the following years:

Blackhill	1886	1906	1919	1921	1923	1934
Passengers	72 915	128 045	190 621	165 771	173 714	40 408

This line was extremely vulnerable to bus competition in later years because the stations which it served were so isolated. Travellers changed their allegiance from the railway to the Venture or the Northern bus companies.

The inevitable reduction in facilities resulted in High Westwood station, which opened on 1 July 1909, closing in May 1942. Shotley Bridge and Ebchester stations followed in September 1953 with Lintz Green in November 1953. Passenger facilities were completely removed from the whole branch in February 1954.

Coal traffic came from Swalwell, Garesfield, Hamsterley, Rowlands Gill, Lintz Green and Blackhill, affecting movement on previously established wagonways and colliery railways. Bricks and timber were transported from Rowlands Gill, milk from Ebchester, and livestock from Rowlands Gill and Blackhill. Freight traffic continued sporadically from 1954 until all facilities were withdrawn on 11 November 1963.

Rowlands Gill station was the last goods depot to remain in use between Blackhill and Scotswood bridge. The track was lifted in 1964 and 1965. After lying derelict for a number of years it was finally opened in July 1972 as the Derwent Walk Country Park, owned and managed jointly by the Tyne and Wear Metropolitan area and, at the Consett end, from Rowlands Gill to Blackhill, by Durham County Council. It is a very pleasant walk, combining the pleasures of the Derwent valley with bountiful supplies of fresh air and beautiful scenery.

2) Lanchester Valley Branch (1857-1966)

This branch line from Durham (Relly Mill junction) to Consett (Derwent ironworks) was built by the NER primarily to convey iron ore from the Cleveland hills to Consett in competition with the Stockton and Darlington railway route through Bishop Aukland, Crook and Tow Law. The Lanchester valley line was granted its act in July 1857, but any initial work was halted almost immediately by the financial collapse of the ironworks' bankers in November 1857.

The works were of such immense importance to the NER and the Stockton and Darlington Railway that both companies gave the works financial aid to keep it going.Survey work was recommended in February 1860 when the ironworks' finances were sorted out, and the construction of a single track line tentatively began twelve months later. The branch was opened for both passengers and freight on 1 September 1862. It terminated at a temporary station called Lanchester Valley terminus until Blackhill station was opened on 2 December 1867. Through services from Newcastle to Durham via Blackhill were then started.

After the ironworks were re-organised as the Consett Iron Company in 1864 the Lanchester line prospered. The busiest part of the line, between Relly Mill junction and Lanchester, doubled between 1874 and 1883. Improvements were made to Witton Gilbert station in 1874, and to Lanchester station in 1875. A new station at Bearpark, initially named Aldin Grange, was opened in 1883

Knitsley station was closed for 'economic reasons' between 1916 and 1925. Regular passenger services on the line were withdrawn on 1 May 1939, though the stations remained open for excursion traffic and freight handling. Witton Gilbert closed completely on 30 September 1963, followed by Knitsley in March 1964 and Lanchester in July 1965. The branch closed completely on the 20th June 1966.

3) Tyne Dock Lines (1859 -1938)

On 3 March 1859 Tyne Dock at South Shields was opened. It could handle nearly 400 vessels and the NER built a number of new lines to serve this developing dock area including the well known four stone jetties that were such a permanent feature of the landscape until they were finally demolished in 1977. A large locomotive shed was built at Tyne dock between 1861 and

1862, and this remained in use until 1967.

Tyne Dock was used for importing iron ore for Consett until 1974. The LNER used giant 4-8-0T tank engines to shunt heavy mineral trains in the Tyne Dock area. In 1938 Tyne dock itself was taken over by the Tyne Improvement Commission who then provided the dockside shunting engines and looked after the dockside lines. The famous Tyne Dock-Consett iron ore traffic was the major reason, it would seem, why the Consett Iron works were kept open for so long. The traffic from there commenced in 1880 although for many years a certain proportion of ore also came from Sunderland. All of the works' ore and most of its coal arrived by train. The ore came from Tyne Dock and the coal from east Durham. Other flows of traffic were fuel oils and the outflow of steel plate.

The Consett-Leadgate-West Stanley-Newcastle line (Pontop line) passenger service was also closed on 23 May 1955. The line from the BSC works at Consett to Tyne Dock was closed shortly after the steelworks itself closed in 1980. Until the Consett works finally closed, a large fleet of diesels worked lines internally with the heavy incoming ore trains sometimes being hauled by close-coupled triple diesel shunters.

Another line with which the Consett Iron Company was involved was the Jarrow Steel works. This major works was opened before the Second World War as a subsidiary plant to the Consett works. By 1979 there was still a half-mile branch, through residential development to the NER/BR Jarrow branch to South Shields and Tyne Dock.

Between their closure in the 1960s, and the late 1980s, Durham County Council was statutorily committed to plan and develop, and at present manages, some 157 miles of former railway lines in the county for the use and the benefit of the community. These include most of the aforementioned former rail links. The Blaydon to Blackhill line was eventually opened to the general public as a linear country park of 330 acres, about $10^{1}/_{2}$ miles long, in 1972.

EARLIER PROPOSED RAILWAY SCHEMES

4) The Newcastle, Shotley and Weardale Junction Railway Proposal

This 1844 scheme was mooted at the height of the 'railway mania' which never saw any development. It was intended to be a link between the Newcastle and Carlisle Railway at Derwenthaugh and the Stanhope and Tyne Railway at Consett, via the Derwent valley.

5) Newcastle and Derwent Valley Railway Proposal (1859-1860)

This proposal followed on from those in 1) above and was intended to run from Scotswood bridge to Hownesgill. It represented a serious threat to the North Eastern Railway as it was backed by the giant London and North Western Railway which was anxious to get a foothold in the lucrative Tyneside coal trade.

The strategy was one by which the London and North Western controlled line from Tebay to Bishop Auckland, and was to be used with transport from Bishop Auckland to Crook and Consett via the Tow Law and Stanhope branches of the Stockton and Darlington Railway. It then continued on the new Newcastle and Derwent valley railway line from Consett via the Derwent valley to Scotswood, to connect with the Newcastle and Carlisle main line.

The North Eastern railway was alarmed by these proposals. It counteracted immediately by preparing a rival proposition for a Derwent valley line, called the Blaydon and Conside Branch, which was submitted simultaneously to Parliament. There was a fierce discussion but the NER won the day, mostly because it had come to an understanding with the Stockton and Darlington railway. The promoters of the above scheme were not content in defeat and tried a second time, without the help of the Stockton and Darlington Railway and failed once again to gain a foothold in the north-east.

6) Newcastle, Derwent and Weardale Railway Proposal (1861-1862)

This scheme was a continuation of the plan in 1) above to link West Auckland with Newcastle via Consett and the Derwent valley. After a prolonged and heated debate in the House of Commons, the North Eastern Railway won again with an alternative scheme. This was to be the last time that the London and North Western Railway was to try to invade NER territory.

7) Stockton & Darlington and Newcastle & Carlisle Union Railway (1856-1864) *(see map 4)*

The exhaustion of the indigenous supplies of iron ore for the Consett and Derwent Iron Company meant that the company had to look elsewhere for its iron ore supplies. Possible sources were the iron ore deposits of west Cumberland and the limestone deposits of the Cleveland hills .

Ore from west Cumberland came to Consett by a very circuitous route. It travelled along the Newcastle and Carlisle railway main line to Blaydon, along the Redheugh branch and up the Redheugh incline to Gateshead, along the ex-Brandling junction railway to Pelaw, on the Pelaw to Washington cut-off and finally along the Pontop and Shields line. A sensible suggestion was to build a direct line from the Derwent Iron works to Stocksfield on the Newcastle and Carlisle railway via Ebchester and Apperley Dene. An Act was granted for this line in July 1856 and work began next to the ironworks a year later. After just a mile had been built all construction work was halted on 1 November 1857, because of a collapse of the ironworks' bankers. When things were finally resolved in 1864, there was little point in resuming construction because by then the NER had begun to build the Blaydon to Consett branch, which also linked Consett with the Newcastle and Carlisle railway main line. The Stockton and Darlington and Newcastle and Carlisle Union Railway was therefore abandoned by Act of 23 June 1864 and Ebchester and Apperley Dene never had their expected rail service. The one mile of completed track at Consett became sidings for the iron works.

SOME DATES CONNECTED WITH THE FORMATION OF THE RAILWAYS AROUND CONSETT

15/5/1834	Stanhope and Tyne and South Shields Railway opened
1/6/1836	Newcastle-Carlisle-Blaydon-Derwenthaugh opened
1/3/1837	Derwenthaugh to Redheugh opened
13/5/1842	Stanhope and Tyne Railway Company dissolved; Pontop and South Shields Railway formed
14/5/1845	Weardale Extension Railway opened
24/5/1847	Newcastle-Carlisle-Swalwell branch opened
31/7/1854	North-Eastern Railways formed
April 1855	Burnopfield and Dipton opened
14/7/1856	Stockton and Darlington & Newcastle and Carlisle Union Railway Act of Incorporation
13/7/1857	NER Lanchester Valley Branch Act
1/7/1858	Hounesgill Viaduct opened
3/3/1859	Tyne dock opened
4/7/1859	Waskerley deviation opened
3/6/1862	Stockton & Darlington Crook-Tow Law Deviation Act
17/7/1862	NER Conside and Blaydon Branch Act
1/9/1862	Lanchester Valley branch opened
13/7/1863	NER Stockton and Darlington Amalgamation Act
10/4/1867	Crook-Tow Law deviation opened to goods traffic
18/6/1867	Blaydon-Conside line opened to goods traffic
2/12/1867	Blaydon-Conside line opened to passenger traffic
2/3/1868	Crook-Tow Law opened to passenger traffic
5/6/1868	Hounsgill-Consett north route opened to goods traffic
1/10/1868	Crook-Consett (Carr House) passengers diverted to Benfieldside, Blackhill
1/1/1886	Annfield Plain-East Castle deviation opened

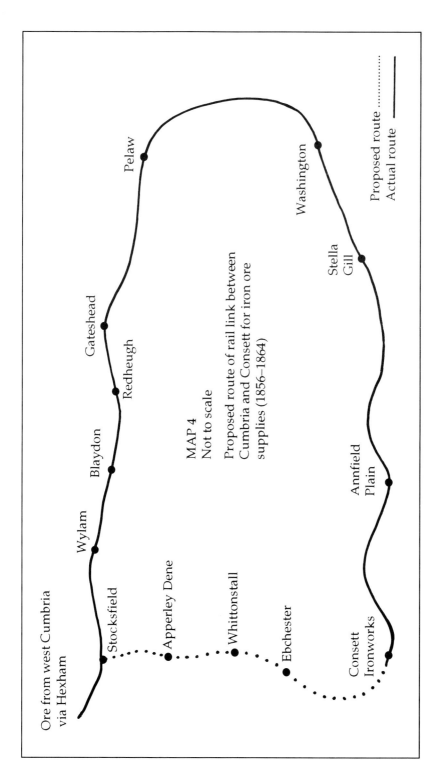

Ore from west Cumbria via Hexham

Stocksfield

Apperley Dene

Whittonstall

Ebchester

Consett Ironworks

Wylam

Blaydon

Redheugh

Gateshead

Pelaw

Washington

Stella Gill

Annfield Plain

MAP 4
Not to scale

Proposed route of rail link between Cumbria and Consett for iron ore supplies (1856–1864)

Proposed route ....
Actual route _____

47

23/5/1887	South Pelaw-Annfield Plain Deviation Act
16/10/1893	Dunston extension and staithes opened
16/10/1893	South Pelaw-Ouston route opened
13/11/1893	South Pelaw-Annfield Plain deviation opened to goods traffic
1/2/1894	South Pelaw Annfield Plain deviation opened to passengers
1/5/1896	Change of name of Consett station to Blackhill, formerly known as Benfieldside station or railway sidings
17/8/1896	Annfield Plain-Consett passenger traffic began
April 1900	Blaydon locomotive sheds opened
29/8/1904	Derwenthaugh branch opened
1/3/1905	Dunston goods station opened
5/1/1908	Blaydon-Consett branch widening completed
1/7/1909	High Westwood station opened
1/2/1916	Knitsley station closed to passengers
13/3/1925	Knitsley re-opened to passengers
11/7/1927	Aldingrange renamed Bearpark
1/2/1934	Shield Row re-named West Stanley
1/5/1939	Blackhill-Tow Law service withdrawn
1/5/1939	Lanchester Valley passenger service withdrawn
9/9/1940	Waskerley and Annfield Plain locomotive sheds closed
4/5/1942	High Westwood station closed
1946	Stanley to Pelton level inclines closed
28/2/1951	Weatherhill and Crowley inclines closed
1/2/1954	Blaydon and Consett branch service withdrawn
23/5/1955	Pontop branch-Newcastle-Annfield Plain-Blackhill passenger service withdrawn
11/6/1956	Tow Law-Crook passenger service withdrawn
11/11/1963	Blaydon-Consett branch closed completely
24/5/1965	Consett locomotive shed relegated to signing-on point
5/7/1965	Wear Valley-Tow Law line closed
2/8/1965	Waskerley-Parkhead (Blanchland) goods line closed
6/6/1966	Rowley goods station closed
20/6/1966	Lanchester Valley branch line closed
29/4/1968	Burnhill-Weatherhill line closed
11/4/1969	South Pelaw-Stella Gill Pelton level to Craghead line closed
1/5/1969	Consett-Burnhill junction line closed
1969	Bowes railway-Pontop to Jarrow line, Marley Hill to Burnopfield and Marley Hill to Kibblesworth line closed
13/8/1970	Marley Hill sidings closed

CHAPTER 3
The Ironmaking Industry

Early types of steelmaking; formation of the iron industry in Consett;
operation of blast furnaces; working conditions; puddling; moulding
and casting iron

BEFORE THE INDUSTRIAL REVOLUTION

The method of crucible steelmaking, invented in about 1740 by Benjamin Huntsman, a watchmaker, was a great advance on the ironmaking of the day. Huntsman had been looking for finer steels to make springs for watches. He had melted shear steel in a crucible or clay pot in an attempt to provide steel which would serve his own business. He was successful, as melting the steel made it more uniform and also allowed some of the impurities to rise off into the top of the slag where they could be skimmed off. The product was known as crucible steel.

Before this method, there had been only two forms of steelmaking, blister and shear steel. Both steels were forms of cemented iron, that is a malleable iron which has absorbed carbon.

The process for making cemented iron was as follows. Malleable iron bars (which were almost free of carbon) were heated, completely surrounded by charcoal, in a furnace at a red heat for from five to twelve days. The bars thus absorbed an amount of the carbon from the charcoal, which could be approximately controlled, and the quality of the charcoal used was of paramount importance. The resulting process produced blister steel, so named because of the appearance of its surface. Blister steel bars were broken into lengths of about 12 inches, which were piled on top of one another, again heated and hammered into a bar to produce single shear steel, used for cutting tools, such as sheep shears and perhaps for the cloth-cutting trades of the time. An especially high-quality of steel was achieved by repeating the process and producing double shear steel, perhaps under a tilt-hammer.

A tilt-hammer was an early adaptation of water power by the force of river water turning a water-wheel which turned a horizontal shaft. This was engaged on a concentric or oval-shaped wood cam. As the shaft turned, the oval shape would cause the hammer to rise and fall on the anvil. The blacksmith or swordmaker could then use both hands for the task he was doing.

One of the best and last of these cementation furnaces in England still stands at Derwentcote, near Shotley Bridge today.

Derwentcote steel cementation furnace, before renovation.

THE FORMATION OF THE IRON INDUSTRY IN CONSETT

Between 1830 and 1870 the ironmasters of Great Britain were able to exploit rapidly developing markets at home and abroad in the fresh atmosphere of relatively free trade. At the beginning of the 1840s the north-east of England was an insignificant producer of pig-iron, but during that decade the ironstone deposits of the county were opened up. Industrial activity in the north-east was much influenced by the local Quaker community, and the foundation of ironmaking at Consett was no exception. Shotley Bridge had been one of the early strongholds of Quaker activity in the north, and the members of the Society of Friends owned much of the property in the vicinity, although many of them had moved elsewhere to pursue business interests.

The Richardson family was one that had remained active within the area. Jonathan Richardson, who developed the spa at Shotley Bridge, was an important figure in the establishment of ironmaking at Consett. He was the Managing Director of the Northumberland and Durham District Bank which figured largely in the formative years of ironmaking in the district.

It was the Shotley Bridge spa that brought William Richardson of Sunderland to the locality for health reasons in the autumn of 1839. During his stay he became friendly with a local cartwright, John Nicholson, who was also an amateur mineralogist. Nicholson showed Richardson some samples of ironstone found 'on the blue heaps at Consett'. Richardson then made preliminary examinations of the area, and called upon Robert Wilson of Newcastle to undertake more exhaustive tests on the deposits, to ascertain whether they were would be viable as an industrial concern. Shafts were dug and samples of ironstone were taken for analysis which was probably carried out by the Quaker ironmasters of Sunderland.

The analysis must have proved satisfactory, as four gentlemen, three of them Quakers, formed a partnership with £10,000 capital, to manufacture pig-iron from the ironstone at Consett. Speculation of this sort was not for the faint-hearted or inexperienced, but for those who had sufficient entrepreneurial drive to grasp the nettle and to forge ahead. It must also be remembered that at the time of the formation of the Derwent Iron Company the concept of limited liability in business had not yet been perceived. The only limit in liability rested with the partner or partners with whom the entrepreneur was associated. He risked most things, if not everything in the markets of the day. On the other hand, however, the rewards for success could be phenomenal.

Jonathan Richardson's commitment was made even more clear by the proceedings of 1840. In that year he was approached by the partners in the prospective ironworks, not to join them, but to purchase the available Consett Estate and lease the mineral rights to the partners. Therefore, although Jonathan Richsardson was never a full partner, he did make a considerable investment which depended upon the success of the ironworks.

The iron company was under agreement to pay Jonathan Richardson royalty rents for the mineral rights. The company had already taken a lease of two royalties, those of Delves and Hounesgill, along with the Consett Estate. This latter was leased from Jonathan Richardson, giving him a vested interest in the size of the iron company. The Northumberland and Durham District bank also was to make substantial loans to the Derwent Iron Company.

The four original partners seem to have quickly appreciated that the location was not ideal for the production of pig-iron alone, and that a greater advantage was to be gained by the addition of forges and finishing facilities. The agreement between Richardson and the Derwent Iron Company stipulated that the ironworks should work the minerals beneath the Consett Estate, paying a royalty on all it took out, and also compensation on any land that was rendered unusable by the dumping of slag.

Coal was a relatively cheap input at Consett, and thus the further that the metal was refined and finished, the greater would be the potential profit. To concentrate exclusively on the manufacture of pig-iron, as the earlier concern seemed to have considered, would leave little room between the cost and market price. However, by further refining and finishing the metal, a good deal could be added to its market value without any substantial addition to cost. This is also thought to be the reasoning behind the foundation of the tinplate industry in the area, of which more will be said later.

Almost immediately after the formation of the company, the decision was taken to expand the plant beyond the two blast furnace capacity to include

Early steel rolling techniques.

puddling and finishing mills. This required a considerable injection of new capital, more than the existing partners could afford. This may have induced them to merge their interests with Redesdale partners, Messrs Bigge, Cargill and Johnson, to form the Derwent Iron Company in 1841. It is thought that at about this time the two blast furnaces could deliver about 230 tons of pig-iron per week.

At about the same time, the new company bought the Bishopwearmouth ironworks, with a ready built puddling plant and rolling mills. This was probably to build up skill and expertise which could be transported to Consett, as the use of the plant at Bishopwearmouth for finishing would no doubt have lost the full advantage of the cheap fuel resources, had the motive been to send the pig iron to Bishopwearmouth. However, after these two mergers the new Derwent Iron Company expanded very rapidly. By 1845, the debt owed to the Northumberland and Durham District Bank amounted to £500,000, and by 1846 the company was being described as possibly the largest ironworks in the north of England.

Problems Considered at the Time

To commence on a sound basis, an establishment consisting of blast furnaces, refineries, puddling forges and rolling mills as proposed, would have required capital of at least £20,000 per blast furnace (including rolling mills, etc.) where four were required. With fewer blast furnaces, a larger amount of capital in proportion would have been requisite (see Appendix II).

All such calculations were necessarily based on the price of building materials, the cost of ironstone, coal, limestone, labour, carriage and other details as applicable to particular localities. A regular and sufficient supply of all materials for the furnaces was necessary, as any delays could cause interruption to the works with consequent losses. Other problems at the outset were the size and power of the various engines needed to operate the works; technology using steam in industry was still relatively new.

Of no less importance was the arrangement of the tramways and inclines; of depositing spoil, cinder and other refuse in places so that it would not have to be moved again at some later date at unnecessary expense. These are but a few of the problems that must have been encountered by the founders of the company.

The provision of labour, both skilled and unskilled, was perhaps the greatest problem of all, combined with the need for sufficient housing for the immigrant labour force. Such was the magnitude of the construction and development of the works at hand, that the danger of under capitalisation could easily have arisen, thus leaving little or nothing for conducting the commercial business of the enterprise. The iron had to be sold as fast as it was produced to meet the current expenses. This tended to make the market price lower than it otherwise might have been. Calculations as to the cost of fuel, ironstone and limestone would not only have included the cost of cutting and raising of royalty and delivery at the ovens, but also a proportion of the outlay for sinking pits, driving levels, erecting pumping and winding engines, and making tramways and inclines.

As capital was expended, all estimates would have included interest repayments on capital and, as had been agreed, compensations had to be paid to Jonathan Richardson for surface damage and refuse dumping on the land. Other necessary calculations would have included wayleaves of railways, etc. and administration costs necessary to the trade, as well as the wages of the workers and expected profits of the owners.

Why Site the Works at Consett?

SOME PHYSIOGRAPHIC FEATURES

It was considered at the time that, of the several factors contributing toward the selection of a site for establishing an ironworks, where all the arrangements and requisite preliminaries were favourable, such as carriage, quality of materials and royalties, the exercise of sound judgement in carrying out works was most important for the enterprise to succeed.

Consett's position in north-west Durham overlooks the Derwent valley at some 880 feet above sea level. The predominantly west winds still whip the exposed reaches of the town.

The original physiographic features of the land which were the reason that the ironworks were sited where they were have now disappeared, due in the first instance to over 100 years of industrial activity on the site, and secondly, by the grading and resurfacing of the site upon the closure of the steelworks in 1980. The gentle slope now seen, looking toward the west from the Consett to Castleside road across the former works site, belies the craggy and steep inclines of the 1840s. Within living memory, stories are told of the steepness of the so-called 'canyon road' leading from Berry Edge down to the works.

Older photographs of the blast furnaces and the General Offices (the 'heart' of the works), show the furnaces built into a hillside and facing west. From Consett, down quite a steep slope, the road led west, past Staffordshire Row. This was a row of workers' cottages adjoining the main works offices. The road continued down towards Consett Hall and the River Derwent about half a mile further to the west. Staffordshire Row, incidentally, was named after the origin of some of the immigrant labour who settled in Consett at the time.

Ordnance Survey sheets of 1856 and 1895 show the degree and extent to which landfill operations took place during only the first fifty years of industrial activity. This was mainly the slags and waste materials from the works, for which Jonathan Richardson continued to receive royalties for quite some time. The wastes were useful in the longer term, as they were used to level the ground upon which further extensions to the works could be built.

The siting of the original blast furnaces and offices will always leave a clue to future generations as to what the original topographic features were like. Another clue lies some distance away in the present day Blackhill Park. The whereabouts and extent of the 'blue heaps', mainly along the line and below Aynsley Terrace in Consett, can be seen by standing on the rugby fields below Aynsley Terrace and looking due east, upward toward the terrace. The waste heaps were put there by mining operations both at No. 1 pit up on the escarpment of Medomsley Road, and from waste disposal from the Mount Pleasant pit, further south toward the heart of Consett. An entirely new picture of the area emerges if one tries to envisage what the land looked like before the mining operations of the 1840s. Parts of a very steep crag still exist on this level, which roughly followed below the escarpment of Medomsley Road to Consett, and diminished towards the Grove and Moorside. The steep slope of Blackhill bank and the vicarage fields toward the west and river Derwent suggest that there were individual outcrops.

The lie of the land quite possibly gave the builders of the first ironworks the idea to use the crag bottoms to site the blast furnaces. This would have been for two reasons. Firstly, the westerly winds would aid the blast air needed to purify the iron. Secondly, the difficulty of top loading a blast furnace, perhaps 45 feet high, was eradicated, as the top of the blast would then be level with the top of the crag into and against which the blast furnace was built. Many people who worked within the BSC works before it closed can remember that the blast furnaces sited on the original ground were built against a steeply rising slope of ground toward Consett.

The local land had hardly been farmed until the mid nineteenth century, explained perhaps by the bare, bleak landscape and harsh environment encountered. There were the Conside buildings and Consett Hall, which were seventeenth-century farmhouses, although there is little evidence that the land had been much worked. Ordnance Survey sheets of 1856 show the area of the works, with Consett Hall overlooking the Derwent valley at the top of Consett Lane (locally known as Muttonclog Bank) and at the foot of the present-day Grove housing estate. Immediately west of the works, fields are shown as being newly farmed, planted and enclosed, in direct contrast to the unenclosed waste and common land surrounding it.

The unchecked Howden Burn would have cut a swathe across the land, to gouge out the hillside in ever greater ferocity, down to Howden cottage and the river Derwent. This became known locally as Stinkey Burn in later years, some say as a result of the smells associated with the tipping of slags nearby.

Economic Reasons

As already mentioned, the coal and iron ore reserves found at Consett were the chief basis for establishing the works. The deposits of iron ore were described as being in a working seam section 7 feet high, with the ore occurring in six or seven bands, each about 12 inches thick. Twenty seven feet below this first seam was another containing a 6-inch band of iron ore.

At the outset this ore could have been worked out for between 7 and 8 shillings a ton, and original estimates of the extent of reserves made by Cargill put the potential output at 5234 tons per acre. Some time later the company's mineral agent found that Cargill had overestimated the reserves, and that they were of poor quality (only about 26 per cent iron). Under the circumstances, the reserves were only economical as long as they were cheaper than the alternative of importing ore from elsewhere.

In retrospect, the partners had no grounds to develop the works as quickly as they did on the basis of such uncertain estimates of the ore reserves. Within a few years, imports of iron ore were arranged from the new Cleveland sites and by 1852 Consett finally gave up the idea of producing its own ores and relied entirely upon imported ores.

The asset which really made Consett viable from the outset was the nature of its cheaply won, top-quality coking coal. One of the reasons why the coal was so cheaply worked was that the royalties were low and this in turn meant that the Derwent Iron Company was able to exploit its position to secure cheap coal. It was often stated that the total cost of coal at Consett was only as much as some other companies paid in royalties.

Between 1841 and 1864 the Derwent Iron Company mines were producing coal at average price per ton of only 2s. 6d. or 3 shillings. It was hardly any wonder that in the years that followed, the Derwent Iron Company, and later the Consett Iron Company, determined to continue a hold on the majority holding of mines in north-west Durham.

The third main material input was limestone for pig-iron making, and this was obtained from the quarries of Stanhope in Weardale. Some of these quarries were purchased by the Derwent Iron Company as early as 1842.

However despite the proximity of the raw materials there remained the need for good communications network, as there was little market for Consett's product in the immediate vicinity. It had to go to the Tyne or the Wear for transport to the customer. It may be seen therefore that the next most important factor was the development of a satisfactory network of communication and transport.

By 1846 the Derwent Iron Company was being described as the leading firm in the north, with 14 blast furnaces and rolling mills capable of turning out 900 tons of bar-iron a week. There were 12 refineries, 22 steam engines to turn machinery, and 35 coal and iron pits to supply materials. These figures make one wonder at the effort needed to bring about these results.

This rapid expansion was due to the large advances and loans made by the Northumberland and Durham District Bank, of which Jonathan Richardson was the Manager. Incidentally, it is significant that at this time bankers were not unwilling to sink their assets in such intractable investments with apparently little regard for liquidity. A striking example of the extent to which bankers sometimes allowed their ironmaster customers to run up huge overdrafts is shown in the relationship between the bank and the Derwent Iron Company.

By 1851 these works were described as the second largest of their kind in the country. In the same year, an iron plate of 20 feet and a section of iron rail of 60 feet was submitted for an order with a marine engineer.

THE BLAST FURNACES OF CONSETT

The exact dimensions and number of blast furnaces which the Derwent Iron Company operated when it first came into production are not known, but a short examination of the blast furnace size of other works of the time can give an estimate of the probable size. By the examination of old Consett Iron Company magazines it would seem that when the Derwent Iron Company first went into production, a weekly production figure of about 230 tons was being achieved.

The Leeds Ironworks of Cooper Field and Hood had built blast furnaces 42 feet high, with two tuyeres (tapholes) and produced 65-70 tons of iron a week. At Brymbo near Wrexham, the height of the blast furnaces was also in the order of 46 feet, with a weekly production of iron of 50 to 70 tons.

The above production figures are quoted as having been achieved by using only a cold blast of air at about 2 or 3 lb pressure per square inch. The blast of air was to aid the chemical reaction necessary within the blast furnace to produce molten iron.

It had been realized for some time that heating the blast air by means of hot air stoves before forcing it into the furnace under (steam engine) pressure, produced a yield of iron that was as much as 50 per cent higher, and the quality was also improved. The hot blast principle in blast furnaces had been

An 1846 view of the Derwent Iron Company from the west.

introduced in Staffordshire and Shropshire. By causing the air to pass through air tubes of heated iron before arriving at the furnace, the blast air temperature could be raised to about 600 or 700 degrees Fahrenheit. This of course had to be achieved close to the furnace. Men would be employed filling the stoves with coal, and boys would rake out and carry the dross away.

Given that the Consett plant of the early 1840s was a new plant, it was at the forefront of ironmaking technology of the day, and would have exploited those 'new' techniques to the full.

Visually, the blast furnace of the day would have greatly resembled a round tower of medieval times, with a square base. The roof was generally flat, sometimes with a rail or gallery around, as this was the means by which the furnace was filled or charged. The coke, ironstone and limestone were brought by barrow to this area for filling the furnace, and there would have been little protection from the elemental weather for those working up there.

In Shropshire, as in Consett, advantage had been taken of the differing levels of ground, and the furnaces were built on low ground, so that their tops were about level with the ground at the higher level. This allowed the coke, limestone and ironstone to be barrow-wheeled to the furnace without much incline. Where the incline to the filling place was too steep for men to barrow the charge, then steam engines were used to pull the materials to the top over pulley ropes and wheels.

The part of the furnace that required repair first was the hearth or lower part. Early blast furnaces had a sandstone hearth before refractory bricks were available. Usually a furnace had to be renewed after about four years.

This cycle of use for the first blast furnaces at Consett perhaps dictated to the ironmasters that expansion of plant was necessary if production were to be continued.

Working Conditions at the Blast Furnaces

The heat, smoke, dust and general cacophony of noise which one would have experienced at the blast furnaces almost defies the imagination. The thump and whoosh of the steam engines, blasting the hot air from the stoves, the roar and crash of the charge materials and the shouts of orders would all have been heard.

At the blast top, the ironstone was calcined or burned before being loaded into the furnace. Alternate layers of ironstone and coke were laid on one another then burned and roasted, perhaps for many days, to drive off unwanted moisture and gases from the ironstone. It was not unknown for young boys to be employed in this work in the early days, filling the boxes and wheelbarrows after the calcining. There were always grown men to direct the work, as the materials could be damaged if they were not correctly handled. The barrow men worked at the blast top. Deep, thinly rimmed wheeled barrows, each able to hold a ton of material, were wheeled and pushed to keep the furnace in operation.

The charging barrows were, in themselves, a masterpiece of design. The thinly rimmed wheels gave little ground resistance and so made the work of pushing a ton of ironstone much easier. However, as the wheel rims became worn and resistance grew, the work became progressively heavier. The short handles on the barrow were placed to aid the fine balance necessary for safe transportation. The men who operated the barrows sometimes loaded them as well, to ensure that they got the barrow correctly balanced. All of these processes took place in the open weather and could be very laborious.

Early blast furnace wheelbarrow for charging the furnaces.

At the blast bottom work never ceased. Sand was arranged on the floor in such a way to ensure that when the keeper of the furnace determined the furnace ready for tapping, a hole could

Preparing fuel for the blast furnaces.

be drilled through the sand and clay at the bottom of the hearth, allowing the iron to run free. The broad runner into which the molten iron first ran was known as the 'sow' and the smaller manageable arrangements in the sand running from the 'sow' were called 'pigs', thus giving pig-iron its name.

After the tapping had finished, the waste materials or slag was run off. The cooled slags were lifted by steam crane onto a bogey for dispersal to the slag heaps, while the pigs and sows were broken by hand and steam crane into smaller pieces for easier handling. The work had to be finished before the next furnace was tapped, as the same men who worked the first furnace would invariably have had to operate the next.

Food and drink were taken as and when it was possible, as there was no set time for breaks. Usually there were two shifts of work at the blast furnaces, from 6 a.m. until 6 p.m. and vice versa. The shifts changed once a week, and this was achieved by the dayshift crew on Sunday working through the night to complete a full 24-hour cycle until 6 a.m. on Monday.

Of the hours and working conditions, it was reported at the time that, even with the long shifts of perhaps 12, 18 or even 24 hours at work, 'there is no evidence that the constitution is harmed in any way'.

The men were fully aware that, in these hellish surroundings, death and injury were never far away. The possibility of being gassed or burned, having an infection or amputation, was ever present.

Perhaps worse than death was the plight of those permanently maimed, finding themselves never able to work again. There was some consolation if family and friends could feed and clothe the unfortunate, or if another breadwinner in the household was able to provide the rent and roof above their head. All too often the new Poor Law of 1834 dictated that if the poor required help, they could go to the workhouse for it.

At the workhouse, the help that they got, in the form of food and shelter for themselves and family, was administered in such a strict and humiliating manner that many people would rather have died. If they were not to become paupers, they needed to find a job, however hard and poorly paid, or perhaps emigrate. Housing was all too often 'tied' to work, and the danger of eviction and slow starvation under such circumstances could never have been far away in the early years at Consett.

Casting pig iron, showing the 'pig and sow' arrangement of the pig-bed.

PUDDLING

To follow Robert Cort's puddling and rolling inventions of the 1780s, perhaps the most important advance in the process was the method of wet puddling or pig boiling perfected between the years 1825-1832.

Puddling was the method of expelling carbon from molten iron to produce wrought iron and was a very difficult manual procedure. It was a batch operation. Each working cycle or heat in a puddling furnace lasted about two hours and produced up to 5 cwt of wrought iron. Two men worked the furnace, a puddler and an underhand, and the work was entirely manual.

The puddling furnace had a hearth of about 6 feet long and 4 feet wide at the widest part tapering to about 20 inches toward the chimney. It was made of firebrick set on edge, or a plate of cast iron covered with a layer of slag, and was sloped to allow the escape of the slags formed during the process of puddling. It was heated by a fire from which it was separated by a bridge 10 inches high. The firebars were movable for the purpose of removing the clinkers; and the draught was determined, through the furnace, by a chimney 30-50 feet high, with a damper at the top which could be raised or lowered by means of a chain or lever.

Openings in the front communicated the grate and hearth; the latter was chiefly used for working the metal with a 'paddle' or iron bar during the process of puddling. Another opening near the chimney was used for charging and cleaning out the furnace. The furnace was strongly built and encased with cast iron.

The charge of fine metal was piled up on the sides of the hearth, until it nearly touched the dome. The centre was left clear for working the charge, and so that the hot air could circulate about it. A portion of rich slag and iron was added; the doors and the damper at the top were closed, and fresh fuel was added to the fire. After about half an hour the metal began to melt and flow to the bottom of the hearth. The puddler would then remove a small iron plate from a hole in the working door, pushing the 'rabble' or long iron bar into the furnace and stirring up the molten metal so as to expose fresh surfaces to the oxidising influences of the draught, at the same time moving it further from the bridge, to prevent the partially melted iron from mixing with that which was well melted.

Typical puddling sheds and furnaces of the day (note the spare 'rabbles' outside the shed).

When the charge had been made into a uniform pasty mass, the fire was lowered by gradually closing the damper and throwing a little water into the furnace. The metal then assumed the appearance of boiling, and escaping carbon monoxide gas burned readily at the surface in a characteristic blue flame.

The metal was constantly stirred with an iron paddle to expose fresh surfaces to the effect of the gases; direct contact with the atmosphere was avoided as much as possible by keeping the working door closed, to prevent the metal becoming too oxidized.

Great strength was needed for this work and also skill, as the puddler had to monitor the rate of decarbonization of the iron using his hands, eyes and experience. By continuing to 'work' the metal it gradually lost its consistency and became 'sandy', or 'dry'; the blue flame would die, but the puddler would continue to work the metal until it appeared uniformly granular. Care had to be exercised at this point otherwise too much of the iron would be reduced, resulting in a poorer quality.

Puddling was acknowledged as one of the toughest jobs in nineteenth century Britain. Puddlers were renowned for consuming enormous quantities of beer. The murderous heat of the forge and the heavy unrelenting physical nature of the work, meant that a good puddler was a much respected member of the ironmaking community of the time. In the hey-day of wrought iron manufacture there were literally thousands of forges throughout Britain.

When the boil in the furnace had reached the critical point, the slag was separated from the iron and overflowed from the stopper hole in the furnace door. What was left was a pasty mass of decarbonized iron, interlaced with slag. The puddler then pulled the partly molten mass of iron onto a narrow iron-wheeled barrow and transported it to the forge hammer. The iron, or 'ball' as it was known, was hammered into a 'bloom'. The bloom was then hammered into shape, a process known as shingling.

The steam hammer drove out most of the impurities during the hammering process, although thousands of strands of slag remained, trapped within the ball of iron. It was this fibrous nature of the slag within the body of the iron which added to the strength and resistance to fracture of the wrought iron, as compared with pure iron. When the forge-hammering was completed, the bloom was lifted on to a barrow, for transportation to the rolling mills to be rolled down to size and section. There was a series of grooves between each roll and by passing the iron through successively smaller grooves, it was rolled thinner and thinner. The remaining impurities were by this means transformed into thousands of parallel threads which strengthened the material even more.

To make the very best quality wrought iron, the bars were chopped and heated to melting point in piles, then by repeated hammering and rolling, they could be made to withstand forces, not just laterally, but in several directions.

Wrought iron's combination of tensile strength and malleability suited it for construction generally. Ships, rails, bridges and steam engines were made using wrought iron, although there were some purposes for which it was found lacking. Steel had the strength of cast iron and the flexibility of wrought iron, and could stand greater strains than the other two put together.

Attempts were made to mechanize puddling but none were successful and it remained a manual operation. The Consett plant introduced steel production in 1881-2, gradually phasing out the process of puddling. A great many puddlers used their skills in other ways within the works. The name still exists today on many a definitive map, showing houses of the earliest form in Consett called 'Puddlers Row'. These stood opposite the present Presto's supermarket and were at the entrance to the ironworks of the time.

MOULDING AND CASTING OF IRON

The quality of pig-iron produced by the blast furnace varied depending upon the type of ironstone and the type of coal or coke used. The pig iron had to be melted a second time to be used for cast iron.

Moulds were made of a mixture of sand and clay in boxes, which were laid on the floor of the foundry. When the iron was melted in a furnace it was let out into large pans, and was carried and poured into the moulds and left to cool. Young boys worked in the foundries to assist the moulder in making the moulds, and to fetch and carry for him.

Early blast furnaces at Consett (note the horse-drawn wagons in the middle foreground).

Iron was graded according to its quality. No. 1 iron was a highly carbonated iron, and was the most fusible and the most fluid when melted, and therefore the best adapted for fine castings, giving a very smooth surface. No. 2 iron was less fluid when melted, but was better for articles requiring strength and durability. No. 3 was used for castings where very great strength was required, but could also be made into bar-iron.

There was a great deal of cast-iron work to be made from the iron directly as it came from the blast furnace, such as water pipes, rails for tramways about the pits, broad flat pieces of iron for the flooring in front of the iron furnaces, and for the flooring of ironworks, and in general articles of a bulky and coarse nature. The labour was much greater for the bulky things, but the principles of casting were the same.

Refiners of Iron

The refinery or refining furnace was generally small, about 3 feet square at the base in the inside. The bottom was of hearth brick, and the front, back and sides were of hollow cast iron, to allow the passage of a constant stream of cooling water flow through them.

The furnace had holes in the sides through which blasts of air, in the same manner as a blast furnace, were admitted. The pig-iron was laid in the refinery with the coke, and blasts of air passed through, causing the iron to melt quite quickly. Two or three hours later the melted metal would be ready to be let off into a mould.

Boys lacked the physical strength to do this work and were used only for bringing and putting on the coke. After the iron had cooled in the mould it was broken into pieces of a manageable size. By 1881-2, the need and use for refineries as described above died out. Conversion of pig-iron into malleable iron without refining by means of the Siemens Martin process of steelmaking had been adopted by then, later to be followed by the Bessemer process.

Other Types of Pig Iron

Some types of pig-iron were unfit for casting because of their poor quality. These underwent other processes to reduce the undesirable constituents so that they could then be made into malleable or wrought iron. They were put into a puddling furnace and then beaten under the forge hammer, and passed through rolls or hollows in two iron cylinders rolling around near to each other, and by that action were forced into long iron bars. They were then cut into lengths by a great pair of shears.

The pieces were then be laid over each other, and heated in a furnace again and again to pass between the rolls again, to form the iron to the shape intended.

Wages

By the 1850s, the ironworkers were in general a better-paid class of worker. In the 1830s and 1840s puddlers earned 5 or 6 shillings a day, and a leading shingler, roller or shearer considerably more.

A sliding scale of wages for the puddlers of Staffordshire had existed since the 1830s and 1840s with puddlers being paid 1 shilling a ton for each £1 in the price of marked bar. Wages in the industry usually followed the price of pig iron and varied greatly between districts and individual works within the same locality. Yet by 1860, and as early as 1850, the applied science of iron and steelmaking hardly existed. Many people concerned with the industry had conducted experiments into the nature and composition of metals, but the amount of theoretical knowledge remained very limited. This was especially true of steel where the nature and compositions of steels were jealously guarded secrets. The production of iron, both pig and wrought, was still regarded as a craft based upon experience and rule of thumb.

Puddling was in no way scientific, but an experienced puddler could virtually guarantee by his character and expertise the quality and value of his product. The quality of the manufactured iron still largely depended upon the knowledge of the puddler, and the skilled men for the most part disliked any threat to their privileged position in the shape of mechanical improvements.

In 1851 when the Great Exhibition was held, the Consett Iron Company sent the following for display at the Exhibition:

1) A railway plate or rail 66' x 9" long, and weighing 17 cwt or 85 lbs per yard

2) A plate for an iron ship, 20' x 42" wide and $7/_8$" thick; weight 11.25 cwt

3) A beam marine engine, 17' 2" long x 4' 8" wide and $1^1/_2$" thick; weight 25 cwt

Each of the pieces was stamped 'Consett Iron Company - Mr George Forster, Manager'.

CHAPTER 4
The Early Coal and Ironstone Mines of Consett

*Names of mines and seams; an insight into early mine working; the
life of the miners; child labour; wages*

SITES OF SHAFTS AND SEAMS

It is interesting to investigate where the first coal and iron pits in Consett
were, and to try and determine the site of those which ultimately determined
the foundation of the town and the formation of the iron and steel making
industry in the area.

As the Industrial Revolution progressed and new techniques and processes
became commonplace, exploration for and exploitation of the area's mineral
wealth also got underway. The fact that iron and coal had been dug in in the
area of Consett for some time was well known. Ironstone deposits in the area
had been excavated in the late seventeenth century by the German
swordmakers, and by 1839, ironstone had been found on the escarpment
between Consett and the No. 1 area of Consett.

In the Teams Valley Mining records office reference is made to Blackhill
Busty seam plan. The old ten-band seam plan under the title of Berry Edge
and Crookhall Royalties is dated 1849 and is a plan of ironstone workings.
This shows an outcrop, midway between Medomsley Road and Consett, and
was the siting of a number pits or shafts which were perhaps instrumental in
the foundation of Consett as a major steelmaking area in later years. These
mines were known as the No. 1, 2, 3 and 4 pits of Consett. Some were coal-
mines, whilst others mined both coal and ironstone.

Nos. 1, 3 and 4 are each dated as having been abandoned by 1849, although
each had both ironstone and coal seams in close proximity to one another.
There is no indication as to when the shafts were sunk other than the date at
which ironstone was found.

The practical notion of being able to mine both ironstone and coal at the
same time was no doubt a great attraction for investment. At the No. 1 pit,
the shaft was situated less than 100 yards from the present roundabout at No.
1 whence the area got its name, at the northern end of Medomsley road. The
pit is seen on the No. 1 seam Berry Edge and Crookhall royalties as being a
coal and ironstone shaft, with both commodities in bands very close to one
another, so that their exploitation would not have been difficult.

The ironstone was described as being a blue plate with balls of ironstone. This was the ten-band seam and was about 7 feet thick at this point and was 30 feet above the Towneley seam (known locally as the Harvey) of coal. The No. 2 pit was only a short distance away and approximately at the edge of the present Belle View football ground. This pit only mined coal. The No. 3 pit was about 300 yards away due south and toward Consett, and roughly where Sherburn Park is situated now. This also mined the ten-band ironstone and the Towneley (Harvey) seam of coal. The No. 4 shaft was near to Hartington Street, and mined the ten-band ironstone, and also the Towneley seam of coal. At the site of the No. 4 pit a borehole was found nearby which indicated that the ten-band ironstone was at 36 feet and the No. 1 ironstone at 67 feet. The depth of these old shafts is not known. There is no trace of these old shafts now, although they are documented in part on the first edition Ordnance Survey sheets of 1856.

Remembering that in those days the newly formed Stanhope and Tyne Railways (Wear Valley Railway, the Stanhope and Carrhouse branch) ran roughly parallel with Front Street and Sherburn Terrace on its way to the South Shields docks with coal and lime, then the tracks would have been iron rails. It is unlikely that the early tramways from the nearby pits had iron rails, as the cost of iron rails before the ironworks were built and in operation would have been extortionate. Wooden wagonways were much more likely.

In the coal-mining areas of north-west Durham, wooden rails and horse-drawn wagons had been used for quite some time. The rails were generally of beechwood with a section of about 5 inches square. For the guidance of the wheels, pieces of wood were pegged on the sides with wooden nails, as a flange. The ends of each rail were sometime later fitted with thin iron plates to ensure a smoother ride, and on the curves of the wagonway to limit the amount of wear of the wooden rail in those areas of greatest use.

Later, when iron was more easily obtainable, but before whole sections of iron rails were a commercial proposition, then a thin iron plate was fitted by men who became known as 'platelayers'. The name has remained to this day for those doing like work on railways.

These wooden rails were about 4 feet gauge and there were passing places along the way. The wagons were made of hardwood and had solid wooden wheels. A very good example of the type of wagon and rail used is displayed to excellent effect at the nearby Causey Arch Country Park near West Stanley.

One of these early tramways ran from what is presently No. 1, roughly parallel to Barrhouse Lane (presently Medomsley road), and connected to Nos. 2, 3, and 4 pits on their way to deliver their loads of ore to the works. The tramway then intersected Medomsley road just east of the Medical Centre, and opposite Gibson Street and ran down what is now John Street and Raglan Street, before turning along the now Albert Road in the region of the Irish Democratic Club toward Front Street. At this point there was a junction to the Consett coal pit about 130 yards due north. This was later to become the site of Consett parish church.

The Blackhill Busty seam plan and the Berry Edge and Crookhall Royalties dated 1849 shows a shaft which is called Consett Coal Pit. It shows Busty seam workings to within 20-30 yards of an old shaft over which the north end of Consett parish church is built. An old ironstone plan shows workings 35 yards from the shaft and the outcrop of this seam would appear to be somewhere near the church. It is probable that any tunnel or excavation at a shallow depth could be connected to the ironstone workings of the No. 1 pit seam, and more particularly the nearby Tin Mill colliery. It is interesting to note that occupants of houses toward Blackhill have found coal outcrops beneath the floor of their houses and this would seem to confirm the above. The shaft referred to was probably sunk to the Busty seam to a depth of about 100 feet.

There were other pits in the near vicinity. These were the Delves Lane pit (then called the Latter-day Saints pit and later the Victory pit). The Delves Lane colliery had a shaft which sank 130 feet to the Busty (4 feet thick) level and also to firebrick seams. This pit employed 123 people and serviced 26 coke ovens in later years.

The method used in the mining industry to denote the depth of a particular shaft, in relation to another without using the name of the seams themselves, was to refer to the horizon of that seam in alphabetical order from the surface. For example, the 'A' level would be nearer to the surface than would the 'B' or 'E' horizon.

Tin Mill colliery, otherwise known as Mount Pleasant pit, was situated at the top of Consett Park and about 100 yards north of the present Derwentside Tertiary college. This shaft mined the Busty seam of coal at 120 feet and the three quarter coal seams at 150 feet, although the depth of the actual shaft is not known. The pit is shown on the first edition maps as being a thriving industry, with tramways leading to the west and downhill to the Shotley Bridge Tin and Ironworks.

The tramways were used for the transportation of coal to the Shotley Bridge Tin and Iron Works at Blackhill, some 400 yards downhill firstly, perhaps by simple gravity feed with the weight of the full tubs from the top pulling the empty tubs from the bottom of the hill to the top on an endless rope. Later steam haulage engines would have been employed to do the job more quickly and efficiently.

Tin Mill pit had two seams at the Busty seam 'Q' level at 4 feet 6 inches plus stone at 120 feet down, with the three-quarter seam at 1 foot 6 inches to 2 feet 6 inches thick at a depth of 150 feet at the 'R' horizon. The actual depth of the shafts is not known. These produced 3000 tons every fortnight

It was reported at the time that the nearby 'Blue Heaps' pit waste site and area was the place where the extent of the ironstone deposits was first realized. Considering the evidence that the Mount Pleasant pit was singularly a coal-pit, and that the nearby No. 1 pit was the nearest ironstone and coal-pit, then this would seem to be correct. A local cartwright and amateur mineralogist, Mr John Nicholson of Shotley Bridge, found samples of ironstone 'on the Blue Heaps' at the top of Consett Park in about 1840. It would seem quite possible that the blue heaps were used as a general refuse tip for the many pits in the area, including the No. 1 pit.

Evidence of the existence of these old pits is now scarce, as the growth and modernization of Consett and its environs has meant the demolition, levelling and eradication of signs of its historic industrial past. The size and area of the 'Blue Heaps' could give the visitor some inkling as to the extent of the operations of the time, and testifies to the extent of the underground workings of the pits. The pithead gear, the tram workings and the pits themselves have all gone, leaving no indication of the industry and hardiness of the folk who owned and worked them. All trace of the Nos. 1, 2, 3 and 4 pits along with the Consett coal pit has gone (although the best possible epitaph could be said to be the building which is built over the latter).

Of the Tin Mill Colliery (the Mount Pleasant pit) little remains to interest the casual visitor to the area. The area is largely overgrown and disused except by the occasional person exercising animals, or perhaps taking a short-cut through the woodland to Blackfyne.

There is still however one interesting relic from those bygone years. Within the woodland there are a number of huge pieces of 'clinker' or conglomerate of some fired material, of unknown origin. The lumps of industrial refuse seem to be common steam engine 'clinker'. Upon close examination, they appear to be burnt or killed shales, bonded together with an oxidised metallic compound. They were probably cleaned out of the bowels of a steam haulage engine which may have operated on the site, for the endless ropes on the tramways or even the pit shaft cage itself.

By 1897 or 1898, the Mount Pleasant pit was gone, the only reference being made is to an 'old shaft' on the Ordnance Survey sheets. The name itself, however, lives on, in the name of a nearby pub.

There were many more shafts sunk at various times throughout the area, some successful as their names are remembered or recorded, whilst others were exploited, abandoned and forgotten as soon as their commercial usefulness waned. The extent of coal ore deposits was without a doubt one of the main reasons for the success of the area for so long. The coal was so abundant and of such high quality as a coking coal, that by 1858 the Derwent and Consett Iron Company was the lessee of 3300 acres of coal royalties.

The company's coal requirements were, by then, mined from four pits on its estates; the Saint pit (so named because it was first worked by Mormons, the Latter-day Saints), Weston, Bradley and Crookhall. Any further requirements were bought from from another pit which worked the Derwent royalties. In the royalty there were four workable seams of which the Busty seam was the most productive; it varied between 4 feet 6 inches and 7 feet high, with another seam above and two below. The coal was ideal for coking in beehive ovens, being highly bituminous and giving a yield of 68 per cent at a very low cost. Indeed a measure of their productivity can be gained from the iron company's output.

By 1858 the ironworks was consuming 600 000 tons of coal, 440 000 tons of ironstone and 110 000 tons of limestone. As the Derwent and Consett Iron Company became bigger and economically stronger, it was essential to its survival that it monopolized the coal industry in the area. As a monopolist, the company caused Consett to become a single-industry town which it was for many years. This brought about difficulties in the social and industrial fabric of the town in future years, that could hardly have been anticipated at the time.

Below are the names of only the major enterprises in which the Consett Iron Company was involved. The list is by no means exhaustive.

PITS OWNED BY C I C

Garesfield Bute		sank	1800	acquired by CIC 1891
Medomsley Busty	sank to Hutton seam		1839	
" "	" " Busty seam		1845	
" "	" " Brockwell seam		1899	
Blackhill Colliery		sank	1840	ceased 1911
Delves pit		sank	1847	" 1922
Eden pit	sank to Hutton		1850	
	sank to Busty		1866	
Black pit Leadgate (Eden)		sank	1844	
Iveston pit (goes back to1611)		"	1850	ceased 1892
Iceston		"	1854	
Derwent pit	sank to Busty seam		1856	
Westwood pit		sank	1871	ceased 1941
Chopwell No. 1		"	1896	
2		"	1906	
St. Ives near Brooms		"	1728	
Saints Pit (later Delves colliery)		"	1745	Crookhall victory pit
No 1 pit Consett	date of sinking unknown ceased 1849			
No 2 pit Consett				
No 3 pit Consett		sank	1847	Berry Edge
No 4 pit Consett		"	1847	
Consett Coal Pit where Consett Parish church stands now				
Marley Hill colliery		sank	1844	
Lanchester colliery		"	1853	
Delight pit Dipton		"	1854	acquired by CIC 1943

By 1894 the CIC had nine pits producing 50 000 tons fortnightly or 1 300 000 tons annually, and by 1921 the annual production of coal had increased to 2 250 000 tons.

AN INSIGHT INTO EARLY MINE WORKING

Coal mining was one of the first major industries in the north-east of England. The early pits were all situated close to rivers for easy transportation and were shallow in depth. By the middle of the seventeenth century the pits had reached a depth of 65 fathoms (390 feet). Horses were used to drain the pits and also to draw the coal to the surface. The steam engine was introduced to pump the pits at the beginning of the eighteenth century. This enabled the pits to be made deeper, but also raised the problems of ventilation.

During the eighteenth century experiments were being made to use the steam engine to haul coal to the surface. At about the same time coal owners adopted screening or sieving the coals. Pits were worked by corves and whin gins. The corfe was a circular basket made of 1 inch thick hazel rods, it had an iron bow for attaching to the hook on the end of the hemp rope 1 inch in diameter. The corfe usually held between 4 cwt. and 7 cwt. of coal. As one full corfe or basket of coals ascended the other, empty, descended into the pit by means of a primitive winding gear, called a 'whin gin'.

A great length of hemp rope was wound around a large wooden drum on a vertical axis. This was called the rope toll. Attached to the bottom of the axle were long wooden bars or levers, to the ends of which horses were harnessed. As the horses walked in one direction, turning the whin gin, a corfe of coal would be hoisted to the surface on one rope end, while at the same time an empty corfe would be lowered at the other end of the rope. At the end of each wind the horses were turned around to reverse the motion of the gin. When the loaded corfe arrived at the pithead it was lowered onto a sledge, detached from the rope and an empty one hung on ready to descend. The loaded corfe was then taken to a gantry high enough to be tipped into a wagon for transport to the river. Eight horses were required to work the gin, two at a time for a period of two hours.

The shaft-tops were at that time unfenced and many men lost their lives by falling down the shafts. As late as 1831 pit cages were not in use, although by 1838 they generally were. Before that time the manner of going down the shaft was by the miner 'putting his foot in the loup' and then being lowered down the shaft on the whin gin. The saying 'keep ahaad' which many will know as the 'pitmatic' way of saying 'keep a hold' is said to have originated in this way.

Generally when men or lads were to ascend or descend, the corves were taken off and the hook was passed through a link in the chain, thus forming a large loop, in which two men each placed a leg. They grasped the chain with their arms, and a little boy would sit astride their knees. He grasped the chain with both hands,and they held him to themselves with their free arms.

Then they were lowered a little until the loops above were filled in the same fashion. Above the top loop 10 or 20 lads would catch the chain, until fathoms of rope or chain, covered with human beings, dangled over the dark abyss of the mine shaft. In this manner they were lowered to the bottom of the shaft.

At the time that the cages came into general use, they travelled between guide rods and carried the iron tubs on wheels, or four miners with bellies touching as they descended into the darkness of the shaft. They were distrusted at first by the miners but were later accepted as a marvel, compared with the time-honoured alternative to descending the shaft.

There were no coroners' inquests on mining accidents in those days. Richard Fines, in his book 'The Miners of Northumberland and Durham', gives some idea of the terribly hard conditions under which the eighteenth century pitman worked.

The pits were inadequately ventilated and explosions were frequent and direful. Boys of tender years toiled long hours underground. Owing to the long hours that they were in the pit, it was impossible for them to see daylight except at weekends. The method of working was very hard on the putters, coals being conveyed from the working places on sledges, carrying a corfe. The sledge had no wheels and was moved on planks of beech wood laid on the floor of the seam and kept in a level position by small pieces of wood. The putting was sometimes done by a couple of boys, one older and stronger than the other.

The stronger boy who was called the headsman shoved the sledge and the younger one who was called the foal, pulled the sledge. He had a belt around his waist to which was attached a chain which passed between his legs and was fastened to the front of the sledge. When they arrived at the crane the single corfe was lifted onto a bogey called a 'rolley' which had four wooden wheels hooped with iron. This carried four corves and was pulled to the shaft by a horse.

In 1777, a great advance was made when John Curr invented the four-wheel bogey and metal plates to take the place of the wheel-less sledge. This man was a good mechanical engineer and inventor of some merit. In 1776, he introduced underground railways, guides on vertical railways in shafts, flat hemp ropes and fixed engines for hauling. In 1802 he was one of the first to build beehive ovens. He died at Sheffield in 1823 and was buried there.

During the eighteenth century ventilation was attained by natural currents from one shaft to another. This was called 'face airing'. Later, a fire lamp was used which was a large brazier suspended in the upcast shaft. This caused a downward current of air in the downcast shaft. In the north of England underground furnaces were in general use, and the shafts were usually topped by a chimney were called the furnace or smoky shafts. In 1835, John Martin proposed to use a fan in place of the furnace. This suggestion ulimately revolutionized the system of mine ventilation.

Up to 1760 the only means of light in the mines was the very dangerous one of naked candles. The steel mill, which was a disc of steel made to revolve rapidly by means of gearing in contact with a piece of flint, emitted a continuous shower of sparks and was invented by Carlisle Spedding, the manager of Whitehaven colliery. It was first used in north Durham at Fatfield in 1763, but was found to be anything but a safe light, and several explosions were traced to its use. However, it still remained in use until the invention of the Clanny, Stephenson and Humphrey Davy safety lamps.

With the coming of the age of steam, great improvements were made to the operations in a pit. Steam-cranes were used for hoisting and lowering the cage in the shaft, and for ventilation purposes. There is evidence that atmospheric or Newcomen's engines were used to some extent during the eighteenth century in north-west Durham, including a coal pit near Brooms which had in it an atmospheric engine in 1728, which was specially adapted to wind coal.

Before the Pea Farm pit closed in 1846 this had a steam winding engine installed. It would not be difficult under the circumstances to imagine that many of the early pits in Consett may also have had steam installed as a source of power.

THE MINERS - AN INSIGHT INTO LIFE

Coal has been mined in north west Durham for many hundreds of years and ironstone for only about 150 years. The social and economic mores of the time, dictated in many ways that greater value lay in land and property than in people. Some sectors of the population were viewed as little more than beasts of burden, for whom little responsibility rested in the hands of society. The individual was responsible for his own welfare and fate.

Early conditions of work in the pits were deplorable, being slavery in all but name. For over 100 years until 1872 there was a continual struggle against the yearly bond. This was a legal device under which the miner was bound under a substantial penalty to work for one colliery for a whole year. He was also subject to various fines and conditions imposed at the owner's discretion, to which the miner had no redress of any kind. Yet there was no guarantee that the miner would even have continuous employment or even any employment at all. Neither was there any agreement regarding rates of pay. The bond was a cause of much dissatisfaction and, in particular, led to strikes in 1765 and in 1810.

The 1765 strike was caused because the mine owners agreed amongst themselves that no employer should take on any man who was unable to produce a certificate of leave from his previous master. When there was a shortage of labour the owner would not give a certificate to a good worker, despite the fact that the pitman's bond was only for a year.

It was not only at work that the mine-owner had it all his own way. He erected the rows of monotonous tied cottages in order to attract the workers he needed for the mines. The employee automatically lost his house if he lost his employment. Indeed this threat was constantly held over the miners' heads and if they took part in strikes many were evicted at a day's notice. If a miner broke his bond, he could be posted in the newspapers as a criminal with a reward on his head. When he was found he was brought back to his master, not to work, but to be denied it by the master, thereby making it probable that he and his family would die of hunger, by being denied work and being evicted from his home.

The people who lived in the houses and worked in the mine were simply instruments of profit and little else.

Houses for the workers were added to the existing agricultural villages. Rows of houses were often erected on virgin land near the pithead. This was done without any respect for the existing form of the traditional village. Pit villages, built around pitheads on the hilltops where the upper seams outcropped, were for the most part, dreary, soulless places and consisted of long parallel, monotonous rows with unmade streets. They were erected as quickly, as cheaply and as close to the mine as possible, with only primitive sanitation and an almost complete lack of social amenities. No real thought was given to the needs of the inhabitants. Thus was the existence of the ordinary mining folk of the eighteenth and early nineteenth centuries.

The gradual increase in demand for coking coal caused by the formation of the Derwent Iron Company led to the opening up of new mines in the Consett area. Miners came from afar, from the many small pits scattered along the west of the county, and even further. Improvements in social conditions were slow, but inevitable. Heralds of change were brought in 1832, when the great Reform Bills of the time were enacted, to be quickly followed by the Royal Commissions into the Employment of Young Persons. These and other statutes were to cause a great improvement in conditions of work and standard of living in the years to follow.

Trade unions, which had been formed but which were denied legality for many years, were eventually given full legal status in 1871. In a few short years, the pitman's bond was discarded as a means of securing labour. Thus ended an era of British social history which should not be forgotten, for the sake of those who worked under such appalling conditions during the formative years of the Industrial Revolution.

THE MINERS OF CONSETT

The miner of the coal or ironstone mines in the times that the town of Consett was being shaped, was a hardy soul, noted and characterized in the eighteenth and nineteenth century by his clothing. He wore boots and heavy woollen stockings, with breeches cut off at the knees and split at the ends so that they could easily be drawn over his boots. A hewer also wore a collarless woollen waistcoat of natural rough felt. He wore this over the top of his shirt and under his jacket whilst going 'inbye' (into the pit), on account of the pit ventilation causing cold surface air to be drawn into the mine. At work he would strip off to the waist and wear the waistcoat next to his skin to absorb the sweat.

Liefchild, a Royal Commissioner into Employment, wrote of the hewers in 1850, 'their pit dress is made entirely of coarse flannel, a long jacket with side pockets, a waistcoat, a flannel shirt, a pair of short drawers,and a pair of stout trousers worn over them. Add to them a pair of hoggers or footless worsted stockings, a tight fitting leather cap and you have a hewer ready for the pit.' The pit 'suit' cost about £1, although many wives made them themselves, out of sheer economic necessity.

Cloth caps were worn, but not helmets until well into the present century. Recollections of old miners indicate that leather caps or helmets were worn by deputies or overseers, but never the pitmen. The word pitman, now rarely heard, is recollected as having been the general term in this coalfield until a few years ago. The word miner has now replaced it.

Pit life was hard in the 1840s. Royal Commissions into the extent of child labour had been set up during these years, although the full effects of their adjudications were still seeping through society in which children of six or eight years of age could work down a mine. Their work, for the few short years that childhood allowed them, must have been a terrifying and bewildering experience, to say the least.

A child of six or even younger could become a trapper, not because of the greed or callousness of the parent, rather because of the economic needs of the family. A trapper opened and closed heavy canvas doors at stategic places in the mine to allow essential traffic to pass, e.g. tubs of coal coming out of the mine or empty tubs going back in. The canvas doors were necessary both to direct fresh air into the workings and, in the event of fire or explosion, they lessened the risk of fire spreading. As the child grew and became used to the pit as a way of life, he progressed to work of a more physically demanding nature. Life expectancy was only about 35 years for the miner, and sometimes a good deal less owing to the ever-present dangers of work underground.

Because of the conditions of work from a very young age, children had extraordinary muscular development, with stunted growth. Ill health as a result of the working conditions often caused early death because of asthma, stone dust, tuberculosis and pneumonia.

Coal was usually free, and house rent was about 3 shillings a week. Any surplus of wages was spent on beer, shoes, clothes and other extraordinary charges. A single man paid 11 shillings a week for board and lodging, washing, mending, darning and marking. He had to pay for beer at the public house, gunpowder, picks, pick shafts, clothes and shoes. Board and lodging only were typically 9 shillings a week.

Typical Weekly Expenses of a Miner with a Wife and Two Children (1850)

Wage: 20 shillings a week	s	d
1 lb. blasting powder	1	0
1 lb. candles for use in the pit		10^1/$_2$
soap		7
1^1/$_2$ lb sugar at 9d a lb	1	1^1/$_2$
2 ozs tea		6
quarter pound coffee		7
21 lbs bread	2	0
yeast, salt, pepper		4
7 lbs. beef at 7d a lb.	4	1
pint of milk a day at 1^1/$_2$d a pint		9
^{3}/$_4$ lb butter	1	1
1 lb cheese		8
1 lb bacon		8
tobacco		8
	14	11

Typically, a trapper could earn about 10d a day, and a driver taking the corves of coal to the shaft, 1s. 3d. a day. The putters and hewers, who were usually on piecework, and were paid on the number of tubs loaded, paid proportionately higher board and lodgings to include the above.

It was understood in society at the time that the miners of the north were a strange class of people, rough, uncultivated and with a great deal of the savage about them. That they were great eaters, drinkers and gamblers and that both sexes were gaudily dressed on Sundays. The women were to be seen on the baking day with their short sleeved dresses showing their brawny arms, as at the public ovens they pass in and out loaves of a size that would satisfy a man's appetite for a week.

So one nineteenth-century observer wrote of the miners.

Generally speaking, the only places for social gatherings for the miners were the church and the pub. The pub usually had a fenced cock pit and a quoit ground at the back, with a quiet place for pitch and toss. These provided the customers with ample opportunities to indulge their taste, with the tap room as their centre. There were often drunken brawls and fighting with all of the demoralizing influences associated with it.

The church on the other hand, had a much more profound influence on the miner and his family, and Sunday worship was compulsory in many pit villages. Even the children who worked were given a grounding in the three 'Rs' long before the days of compulsory education. Sewing and dressmaking classes taught the young girls and wives how to be ever more economical in the home. The men themselves were encouraged to join the temperance league and swear off the demon drink. Despite what others may have thought of the work and lifestyle of the miner, sobriety was not as foreign a word to many of them as was supposed.

Such was the environment of a miner. With toil often pregnant with the pent-up forces of danger, the miner was from his very birth and boyhood, familiar with the darkness and monotony of pit life. Although that familiarity often led him to the discharge of his duty under circumstances from which the untrained would have drawn back, he was neither so reckless of the danger nor so thoughtless of the consequences as might be supposed. There were and are reckless miners, as there are reckless fellows in any walk of life, who would unnecessarily risk their own lives and of those about them. But the miner, as familiar as he is with danger, is possibly a breed apart from the rest.

CHAPTER 5
The Shotley Bridge
Tinplate and Iron Company

Formation of the tinplate works; factors of production; recruitment
of labour; practices in tinplating; tilt hammers; pickling; annealing;
closure of the works and merger

It may seem ironic to some that the site of one the original industrial enterprises which made Consett famous throughout the world, the fitting and engineering workshops, is all that is left after the closure and demolition of the BSC works at Consett and Blackhill. Presently occupied by the Consett Engineering Company Ltd, manufacturing specialists in large and heavy steel fabrications, the site is a part of the Park Road Industrial Estate of Blackhill. A photograph of the actual site is to be found at the end of this chapter.

Shortly after the formation of the Derwent Iron Company in 1841, the decision was taken to diversify production to include those products for which greater profits could be expected. It was soon realized that producing only pig iron was not a feasible proposition because of a number of factors: the isolation of Consett, the limitations of its natural ironstone deposits and the state of the growing British market.

The formation of the tinplate industry in the area could also well serve to give a better understanding as to the type of men who were to become the base stock of the early years of the Derwent Iron Company and later the Consett Iron Company.

With advances in technology, pig-iron was easier to make. There was then a great surge in industrial activity to embrace those industries allied to the iron trade.

The tinplate industry was one such industry in which attempts to revolutionize manufacture were made in parts of Great Britain other than in those areas of its traditional manufacture. By 1800, the tinplate industry, small in scale and subsidiary to the iron industry, was securely established in Great Britain. Using the rolling process to produce blackplate, the industry was able to make tinplate more cheaply than its continental rivals, and as a result, was able to export to new markets both in Europe and in America.

Cheap iron and tin and the rolling mill method of production gave the British industry its position of dominance. The rising standards of living during the early and middle of the nineteenth century and the cheapening of some types of tinplate articles, itself led to an increased demand for tinplate. Between 1800 and 1891 the industry grew rapidly and its output expanded nearly 150 times, mainly as a result of this demand, particularly from the then new industries coming into being as industrial technology developed.

Typical new uses included enamelled goods and wrought iron, bars, wares, tin trunks, cash boxes, baths and tea urns. Tinplate was also used in the dairy industry, for equipment and milk churns and for sugar refining machinery and for the canning of foods at home. The consumption of tinplate in the United Kingdom therefore rose from 1500 tons in 1805, to 9000 tons in 1837, and 12 000 tons in 1850. Tinplate sales overseas increased more rapidly than at home. In 1805, 2500 tons of tinplate were exported, rising to 9000 tons by 1837 and to 25 000 tons by 1854. The number of workers in the tinplate industry rose from 1000 in 1800, to 4000 in 1834 and 5200 by 1851. To a large extent labour was recruited locally.

Between 1800 and 1850, 33 new tinplate works were erected. There were 12 in the Midlands, 19 in south Wales, Monmouthshire and Gloucestershire, and two in the north of England: one at Consett in County Durham and the other at Workington in Cumberland. Among those who financed early tinplate works, two groups were dominant:

1) The ironmasters who were interested in securing an assured outlet for a proportion of their production.
2) The iron merchants who as a result of their knowledge of the state of the market, were eager to secure supplies of tinplate.

Jonathan Richardson, Managing Director of the Northumberland and Durham District Bank and promoter of the Derwent Iron Company, was one of those entrepreneurs who was interested in securing an assured outlet for a proportion of his production. He became the owner and Managing Director, upon its formation, of the Shotley Bridge Tinplate and Iron Company, the only tinplate manufacturing centre ever to be created in County Durham. The entire works are believed to have cost Mr Richardson in the region of £25,000 to build, install the necessary machinery and import the skills necessary to ensure the success of the venture.

The Shotley Bridge Tinplate and Iron Company had origins that were not so far removed as those of the Derwent Iron Company. It is believed to have begun production shortly after the formation of the Derwent Iron Company in 1840, and ceased production of tinplate in 1863. It then became known as the Shotley Bridge Iron Company. It continued in the production of iron for a further three years after which it was then merged entirely with the newly formed Consett Iron Company.

SITING THE WORKS

Historically the tinplate industry had grown as a subsidiary of the iron industry, where coal, iron, and labour skilled in metalwork were available. Within both the Midlands and the two areas of south Wales where tinplate working was traditional, the exact site chosen was often the result of a more or less chance decision by the manufacturers. The primary factor determining the location of a tinplate works was the availability of water power. Although the dependance on water was lessened with the invention and use of steam power, the industry was never able to liberate itself from its need for water, as supplies were also needed for cleaning purposes, for pickling and for storing plates before tinning.

The reasons for siting the tinplate and ironworks at Consett are not really understood, although a few logical assumptions reduce the factors to a minimum. The ready abundance of coal and of iron are well known. The water was supplied from reservoirs installed near and adjoining the works at the bottom of Blackhill bank. These were situated about 180 yards due south of the junction of Park Road and Laburnum Avenue at Blackhill. Although they have long since been filled in and levelled, local maps as late as 1921 show their location and indicate them still being used as cooling ponds.

The Blackhill colliery nearby and Tin Mill pit some distance away were connected by tramways to bring fuel for the steam power and heating. Road links for ready access for the transport of pig-iron from the Derwent Iron Company only some 250 yards distant to the south, were also laid. This was to become the 'Tin Mill Road' which is still well remembered, although now partly covered by the demolition and resurfacing of the modern steelworks plant of recent years.

It is believed that the Shotley Bridge Company laid this road for two reasons. It was decided at an early stage in its history to buy ready manufactured pig-iron from the Derwent Iron Company rather than manufacture its own. This made economic sense, as the iron company could produce pig-iron more cheaply than the tinplate company, and Jonathan Richardson had interests in both companies. Because of the necessary communications and transportation of materials between the two companies, Tin Mill Road was laid. In addition to the above, Tin Mill Place is still well remembered as workers' cottages lining the route, as well as the 'Tin Mill school', as Blackhill Infants' school was known locally, all lending to the memories of the tinplate industry of the last century. Incidentally, the last mentioned is presently used by the locals as the Blackhill Community Centre.

LABOUR AS A FACTOR OF PRODUCTION IN THE TINPLATE WORKS

Shotley Bridge had ironworkers and general labouring skills, but none of those tinplating skills which were demanded in the new industry. Therefore artisan tinplaters had to be imported to the area, whereas that work in the tinplate industry which was of a labouring non-artisan type could be filled by the local population. In addition, the growth and demand for labour of any kind for either industry was such that it could not be satisified by the local population alone. Therefore it had to be imported from wherever it was available.

Since the profitability of the works depended to a great degree on the skill of the workers, competition for key men was fierce, particularly for mill managers, rollermen and tinmen. It was not unknown at the time for managers when looking for other employment in the industry to state 'if you'd be so kind as to employ me I could bring first class workmen along with me'. Thus the personal element in recruitment continued for many years.

The labour employed in the tinplate industry could be broadly divided into two groups, the process workers, who were engaged directly on the manufacture of tinplate in the mill or the tinhouse, and the day workers and maintenance men, who included boiler firemen, locomotive drivers, engineers, carpenters and the like. Apart from the key workers the labour was immobile and rarely moved more than a short distance. As the proportion of skilled workers in the tinplate industry was high, perhaps as much as about 25 per cent of the total employed, it still compared well with 30 to 40 per cent in the large integrated ironworks of the time. This meant that securing sufficient skilled labour in the tinplate industry was not as difficult as in the ironworking complex.

The skills of the labour force had to be recruited from other regions of the United Kingdom. Therefore it may be seen that, as long as the skilled labour of the right calibre were recruited into the area and kept, the immobile stock of semi and unskilled labour of the area could satisfy the needs of the tinplate works. To a large extent, the industry could have been seen as self-perpetuating, as the ruling practice of recruitment of process workers was promotion by seniority.

Generally speaking, new entrants to the industry normally started with one of the simple jobs such as cold roll boy, list boy or grease boy, and were then promoted. This promotion was either to the mill or the tin house, when a vacancy occurred within the mill team itself. In the mill promotion was from behinder to furnaceman, then to doubler, and finally to rollerman and in some cases to shearer. The shearer acted in effect as foreman for a number of mills. In the tinhouse promotion was from list boy to riser, then to washman, to tin man and finally to assorter, who acted as foreman in the tinhouse. Workers learned their next job by watching those with whom they were working and then by practice. A system of seniority applied within a works so that a skilled newcomer might sometimes be required to take a job less skilled than that which he had practised previously.

Women and young girls were employed in some of the relatively lighter jobs, such as opening the plates after rolling, pickling, cleaning and packing.

Evidence from the 1841 and the 1851 census returns (see Appendices IV, V & VI) shows the great number of skilled and semi-skilled tinplate workers who came from those regions of the United Kingdom where tinplate manufacture had historically been more traditional than in the north-east, to ensure the future of tin, and later, ironmaking in the Consett area.

TYPICAL PRACTICE IN TINPLATING

Until the age of steam, the only machine used in an ordinary ironmaking forge was the tilt hammer; it was used to beat the bloom when it came from the finery, and to beat the iron into bars, for example down to one inch square. Now these bars served their purpose well for smithing work, although for the nailsmith and for drawing into wire, they left a lot to be desired.

The plan adopted was to produce a long wide strip under the hammer, which was sheared by hand into a number of narrower strips or rods. After a while, the shears were replaced by circular cutters at the time of water power; these circular cutters became known as the slitting rolls and continued until well into the nineteenth century when the art of rolling had advanced so far that small sections could be made by rolling.

By the mid nineteenth century the tinning of wrought iron was carried out in the following fashion, and was effected by immersion. The most important form of the operation was making tin from ordinary sheet iron (making what was known as sheet tin). The iron plates were carefully cleaned with sand and muriatric or sulphuric acid, and lastly with water, and were then plunged into heated tallow to drive away the water without oxidation of the metal. They were next steeped in a bath, first of molten ferrunginous, then pure tin. They were then taken out and kept suspended in hot tallow to enable the surplus tin to run off. The tin of the second bath dissolved iron gradually and became fit for the first bath. To tin cast iron articles they had to be decarbonized superficially by ignition within a bath of ferrous oxide (powdered haematite or similar material), then cleaned with acid and tinned by immersion as explained above.

So it was thought to have been in the Shotley Bridge tin and ironworks between 1841 and 1863.

OTHER PRACTICES USED IN THE PROCESS OF TINPLATING

Many of the descriptions of tinplating processes to follow are likely to have been used at the Shotley Bridge Tin and Iron Company, although there is little evidence of the actual processes used in the tinplate works. The descriptions therein are intended only as a general guide as to the usual procedures employed in a typical tinplate works of the time.

Pickling

The cleaning process of plates was known as pickling. This was necessary to prevent scale, or the surface formation of metallic impurities which occured in the open air, if the plate was not treated. If an untreated iron plate was tinplated, then the metallic impurity formed under the tinplate could lift the surface of the tinned area, rendering the tinning process useless. To eliminate the formation of scale, many processes were involved. The method in 1820 for black pickling, was that spirits of salts or 'marine acid' were mixed with two pints of acid to three gallons of water. For white pickling, the plates were immersed in the lees of fermented bran for 24 hours, and then steeped in a bath of two pints of vitriol to two gallons of water for four hours, after which they were washed in water and scoured with sand. They were then ready to be dipped into the melted tin, which had a layer of grease or other suitable material on top of it. By 1829 the use of sulphuric acid was patented for black pickling.

In a specification of 1855 for preparing iron plates for a coating of copper, (which allowed the better adherence of tin in a later process), the plates were first given a coating of lead, for which they were prepared by being dipped in an acid solution and washed, then dipped into a lye of caustic soda, and then placed to lie in lime for several weeks.

In these processes the plates were placed together in the bath, and had to be moved by tongs to ensure that acid came into contact with every part of the surface. The use of warm acid instead of cold was suggested in 1837 by Booker, the acid being contained in a lead bath placed in an outer casing with the space between them filled with water heated by a furnace. This specification also mentions the plates being placed on their edges in a rack or frame, and so kept apart, although it was not until many years later that cradles were generally used.

Although in Parnell's patent of 1817 the proportion of acid to water is given for black pickling as one in twelve of hydrochloric, and for white pickling as one in eight of sulphuric acid, a patent in 1863 was granted for the use of a weak sulphuric acid bath instead of a strong one, the loosened impurities being removed afterwards by grinding or scraping.

Annealing

When cold worked metal needs to be softened to permit further working or for service, the metal is heated to cause recrystallization. The heating treatment is known as annealing, although this term also has other meanings. In the early days of tinplate making the plates were annealed, before and after cold rolling in an open furnace.

Tinning

Although the dipping process with the 'brushing' to tin the plates continued at some works until the 1890s, the use of rolls in the tinpot was proposed by Morewood and Rogers in 1843. The rolls were arranged so that the molten metal was kept in contact with the rolled surface. In this patent, chloride of zinc as a flux is mentioned and its method of manufacture described. In the following year, Morewood took out another patent for terne plates, using lead or lead alloyed with not more than 15 per cent of tin, using a flux of sal-ammoniac and chloride of zinc. The name terne first appears in a patent of 1858. In their patent for sheets coated with an alloy of tin and zinc in 1846, Morewood & Rogers describe the coating of the sheets by means of rollers immersed in the bath of molten metal. They also refer to the sheets after coating being passed through rollers immersed in the flux, palm or rapeseed oil.

In 1852, another patent was granted to Morewood & Rogers for coating plates with lead. The pot was made with a division at the top, the molten lead on one side of the division being covered with zinc through which the plate was immersed, and, after passing under the division bar, was raised on the other side. A suitable flux was to be used. At the same time another patent suggested that the coating of the plates could be attained by using three rollers in the bath. The plates descended into the bath on one side of the middle roller and ascended on the other.

Cleaning Machines

The tinplates were, from the earliest days of manufacture, freed from grease after coating by cleaning with bran by hand. In 1861, and only two years before the tinplate works ceased production, a patent was granted for a polishing machine with nine pairs of rollers. The second pair was covered with carpet or other coarse woollen fabric, the other even pairs were covered with sheepskin, and the odd pairs were guide rollers. 'Sharps' or abrasives were supplied from hoppers over the polishing rollers and were brushed off the plates by brushes between the rolls.

THE CLOSURE OF THE SHOTLEY BRIDGE
TIN AND IRON COMPANY

The reasons for the closure of the works and its subsequent takeover by other interested parties, including many who were understandably involved with the then recently formed Derwent and Consett Iron Company, can only be guessed at. One reason would seem to be that, as the national tinplate industry had grown with demand, so the price of the ore necessary for the production of tinplate had risen.

When the tinplate works had been envisaged in the heady days of the early 1840s, the ready access of the raw materials of production were relatively cheap. Abundant stocks of local coal were priced at about 2s. 9d. a ton, with iron ore from the local fields at perhaps 8 or 10 shillings a ton. Although these two remained somewhat stable in the years to follow, the average price of tin ore per ton rose from £77. 8s. 4d. in 1849 to £111. 11s. 8d by 1853. This rise in raw material costs peaked in 1857 with a price of £137. 1s. 8d. per ton. In 1863, the year in which the Shotley Bridge works ceased production, the price had fallen somewhat to £120. This fall continued and by the year 1866, when the works were finally merged with the newly formed Consett Iron Company, the cost of tin ore was only £82. 10s 0d (see Appendices VII & VIII).

Over the same period, the price of finished tinplate remained remarkably stable, and hardly reflected the rise in raw materials. Indeed in some years, prices of finished tinplate can be seen to have fallen in relation to the added cost of tin ore of the time. This would have depressed the markets and, in order to remain competitive, could have depressed wages, especially at Consett. As a further result, many skilled workers may then have looked to changing their employment, quite possibly to ironmaking. In turn the shortage of skills would have had an adverse effect upon the quality of finished tinplate (see Appendices VII and VIII).

This would seem to indicate that the market was becoming a fiercely competitive one in an ever-increasingly technical industry. As a result those works which were better situated geographically or better equipped by either skill or investment, gained the lion's share of the market. The added costs incurred by the Shotley Bridge firm for raw materials and transport, because of its isolated geographic position, denied it the investment necessary to keep abreast of the market.

As previously indicated, the workmen with skills in the tinplating industry at Consett would have had little difficulty in adapting to ironmaking when the tinplate function of the works ceased. There was continuity of skilled labour in the area. This added to the quality of skill and an enrichment of the cultural ties of the people, as well as to the manufacture of iron.

Soon after the Shotley Bridge Tinplate and Iron works were closed, people interested in the ironmaking side of the business got together to form the Shotley Bridge Iron Company. The buildings were leased from Jonathan Richardson, and on 28 July 1863 the first general meeting of the company was held at the Kings Hotel, Darlington. Among those present were ironmasters Isaac Wilson, James Morrison, Robert Dickenson, David Dale (later for many years a Managing Director of the Consett Iron Company), William Barrat, William Whitwell, Thos. MacNay, O. S. Flintoff, J. A. Bush, A. E. Tregelles and W. H. Renwick.

A deed was signed, investing the company, the Shotley Bridge Iron Company, with all the stock, book debts, etc. and indemnifying the Trustees of Messrs. J. B. Richardson as vendors, against all claims in respect of their trust. Among other things discussed were salaries and administrative matters. At the directors' meeting of the same day, it was decided that David Dale be requested to sign all bills and cheques, pending a full consideration of arrangements for directors.

Upon careful inspection of the works and consideration of their requirements, the erection of about fifteen new puddling furnaces and a steam hammer was authorized. The desirability of a new steam hammer for the plate mills was carefully considered, as the type to be bought was one of eight tons weight with a six-foot stroke. As work and modernization continued, the works prospered for a while. The bankers of the Shotley Bridge Iron Company, J. B. Backhouse, arranged the purchase of the 280 acres of land surrounding and upon which the works was situated, and Jonathan Richardson's interest in the royalty held by the company under him. The deal was also subject to the lease of the buildings and works built thereon, exclusive of the mineral rights under the land. The sum agreed upon was £30,000, suitably reduced to take account of other benefits which Jonathan Richardson would have enjoyed, had the full amount being paid. These included the rents on the buildings in which he lived, the works rent, as it was at the time only leased from Jonathan Richardson, and so on. The reduced sum was set at £425 to be paid bi-annually for $14^1/_2$ years at 5 per cent, the total figure being in the region of £17,000. The proposal was accepted and confirmed on the 1 August 1864.

Works and plant expenditure, including the puddling furnaces and patent hammer, an independent puddled bar shears, new, more powerful plate mill shears, a punching machine and the erection of a roof over the loading wharf, were to cost the company some £16,000 over three years.

Like many other industries of its day, the Shotley Bridge Iron Company was not without its difficulties, especially with the awakening of the newly created trade union representations of the workers. Management skills were as vital then as now to enable good relations with the workers. An agreement was entered into with the Consett Iron Company to supply the works with ready-made casts of pig-iron. This would have the advantage of reducing costs, as the pigs could then be directly reduced to a finished product. However, owing to the vagaries of the market, this was at times found to be counter-productive to the Shotley Bridge Iron Company's interests. As the price of iron rose, so did the price of the pig-iron.

The Board of Directors had, from time to time, discussed the expediency of seeking to amalgamate the company with its giant neighbour, the newly formed Consett Iron Company. Proposals were therefore set out, indicating the size of the Shotley Bridge Iron Company's holdings. These being offered to the Consett Iron Company included:

To pay Messrs. Backhouse in the manner described above in respect of Jonathan Richardson	£30,000
For Shotley Bridge Iron Company, shareholders	£13,041
To retire the Shotley Company's acceptances	£21,761
TOTAL	£65,000

Included also was the Consett estate amounting to some 262 acres, allowing annual rents of some £400; the colliery (on lease until 1884), which included the pasture drift seam, the Busty seam and the Brockwell seam, estimated in total to hold some 1,250,000 tons of coal; and the ironworks. These consisted of 42 puddling furnaces, which turned out 430 tons of puddled iron per week, including during periods of strike. There were three plate mills capable of turning out 350 tons of plate per week. Other descriptions include that of boilers, excluding two reserve hand-fired ones, all placed above the furnaces and driven by the furnaces' waste heat. Others were of patent steam hammers, plate shears, scrap shears and puddled bar shears and the covered loading wharf with steam-crane, small fittings, blacksmiths' and joiners' shops, and storehouses and reservoirs. In all, these many and varied skills amounted to a near fully integrated works of the day.

Indeed, the Directors of the Shotley Bridge Iron Company commented in a report at the time that, all things being equal, the works were one of the most economical in the north of England. However, the Consett Iron Company's view and counter proposal indicated that an offer of £55,000 was more in order. This was discussed by the directors and shareholders of the Shotley Bridge Iron Company at an Extraordinary General Meeting on 1 October 1866 and was accepted.

The reasons for the merger was largely to do with the market forces of the day. When the Shotley Bridge Iron Company was formed in 1863, it had only two competitors in the north of England for its product. By 1866, this had grown to ten. Another factor was the state of the market. Because of the lack of capital, many of its customers found they could not meet their commitments, due to a severe commercial crisis. This caused losses to the company by way of irrecoverable bad debt.

There ended one of the more poignant moments in the history of the industries of Consett. The attitudes and motivations of those present at the time can hardly be criticized, as their efforts were to survive and prosper for many years to follow. It is enough to say that those buildings which remain are a symbol of Consett's past successes and hopes.

Consett Iron Company general offices, built 1885 and demolished following the closure of the steel works in 1980.

CHAPTER 6
Social Issues

---

*Early churches; employment of young children; environmental health
and housing; the truck system; social unrest and riots*

A LONG AND EVENTFUL LIFE

On the south banks of the Tyne, four miles west from Gateshead, stands
Whickham village in the county of Durham. In that village I first saw the
light of day having been born about a stone's throw from the Parish
Church, on the 26th October 1821. For the first thirteen or fourteen years
of my life, I spent my time there. As far back as I can remember my
parents kept a school, father having the boys and mother the girls. But
when I was about eight or nine years of age my father gave up the
school, and commenced as carrier between Whickham and Newcastle on
Tyne and took me along with him to help him. Besides that I had to ride
a fine white ass to Gateshead Post Office every morning (except
Sundays) for letters, leaving home at 6 in the morning and returning at 8.
After two hours, off with father again at 10.

When I was about thirteen or fourteen years of age he gave up the
carrying and the family removed to Swalwell, I being the eldest of six,
two boys and four girls. My Father had, before removing already found
employment in the old established factory of Crowley Middlington
where he continued till it closed. But as soon as we got to Swalwell I still
found plenty to do with the horse and cart, which we kept for some time.
After selling the horse and cart I found work in various ways, first in
foundry then in smiths shops. At last I got to C. Middling and continued
to work smiths work in one of the ———? shops, until I left for we were
working only half time, I wandered about for some time seeking work
and at last set off to Consett or (Berryedge as it was then called.) There I
found work at Earl and Dickensons ———? brick Works. Being known to
Joseph Pescod the manager he set me on to fire the kilns at nights, but
lodging was difficult to get. Few houses were built and many a family
went into one before either windows or doors were put on. Mrs Pescod
however got me shelter with the engine man, his wife and two sons who
occupied a single room under the office.

*Extract from an original manuscript of Joseph Surtees Nicholson
(1821-1903)*

J. S. Nicholson continued working in Consett for the rest of his life, becoming a Methodist lay preacher and a businessman. He founded the first Spiritualist church in the area.

(Reproduced with the kind permission of Mrs Margaret Crick of Blackhill.)

EARLY CHURCHES OF THE AREA

The erection of many churches in north-west Durham was largely a result of the industrial growth of the area in the mid-1800s. People brought with them their own forms of worship, at first they formed and gathered at house prayer meetings, having no formal church. The support, organization and building of a church can perhaps best be understood in the terms of the numbers of people involved in those days.

The first religious meetings to be held in the area were by the Quakers, as early as 1653. Later, and before industry had fully opened up the area to the general populace, came those of the Primitive Methodist faith in 1821, to be shortly followed by those of the Roman Catholic faith.

It was decided to cover only those denominations for which there was evidence of them practising in the area between 1839 and 1851. I apologise if I have thus incorrectly excluded any denominations.

One of the earliest headstones to be found in Blackhill Cemetery. It carries a story that everyone should read.

The Society of Friends Meeting House, Shotley Bridge

Before 1730 there were Friends or Quakers living in the Township of Newbiggin by Blanchland. They chiefly belonged to a family called Makepeace, and appear to have been living in that district from 1665. In 1790, the date which the present building bears, a Meeting House was built, at the top of Church bank along Benfieldside Road, presumably on the foundations or site of an even older building. In 1843 the Friends erected a new Meeting House at Snows Green and the old one was converted into cottages, owned by the Piele family. The ground behind it was retained as a graveyard.

For many years the Quakers had this small simple Meeting House at Snows Green and it is believed to have been partly demolished about 1942. It is said that, of the two cottages at the top of Church bank, that it was held on a 99 year lease, but before it expired the membership had so declined that it was closed in 1877, and from that date to the present they have been used as dwellings. The burial ground was also on this site and the last funeral to be conducted in this beautiful graveyard is believed to have been that of Dr Henry Piele.

The Methodist Church, Blackhill and Shotley Bridge

The Methodist movement was founded in 1729 and the doctrines are substantially those of the Church of England. The first 'camp' meeting was held on the side of a mountain at How Cop, Staffordshire. The movement soon spread. In the period from 1740-1750 John Brown, a farmer from Tanfield Haugh became the first local preacher in the north of England. In the years immediately to follow, the great founders, John and Charles Wesley preached in the region and first visited the area in June 1772.

In the early years of the movement, however, the Methodist movement broke up and formed a number of independent bodies such as the Wesleyan Methodists, the Primitive Methodists and others. It was many years before each of these bodies again reunited to form the present Methodist Church. During those years in which they were separate, and indeed since their reunification also, the determinations, commitments and enthusiasms of those concerned have been both incredible and magnificent, when one realizes the benefits which were brought to the ordinary people of the area. This was seen in the organization of classes for the poor, many of whom yearned to read and write. Their doctrine of sobriety, abstinence, hard work and concern for the care and enrichment of the family unit were all of great benefit to the community.

Their early efforts are seen today in the number of churches in Consett, Blackhill and Shotley Bridge which had their foundations in those early years. Hugh Bourne (1772-1852), a country carpenter, was the founder of the Primitive Methodism denomination in 1812, and introduced it into the county of Durham in 1821. The first Primitive Methodist preacher to hold a service in the Derwent valley was a Mr Jersey who preached at Shotley

Bridge and Ebchester in 1822. Methodist services were held at Shotley Bridge in the late eighteenth century in a room near the flour mill.

A very humble church was built in 1814 in a garden given by Christopher Oley, the swordmaker whose ancestors were said to have suffered religious persecution in Solingen in Germany. It was described as being little bigger than than a third-class railway carriage, but it was enlarged in 1839 and replaced by a much more commodious 'chapel on the hillside' in 1855.

Cottage worship began in Blackhill about 1840 in a house opposite the modern day church on Durham Road. A small chapel was built in Derwent street in 1849, but was superseded in 1872 by the much bigger chapel in Durham Road which was opened by the Reverend Peter McKenzie. The original church was sold to the good Templars and still bears the inscription 'Sons of Temperance Hall' dated 1879. It is presently in use as a theatre workshop in Templar Street.

Between 1849 and 1852 the Methodist circuit stretched from Crawcrook to Tow Law and from Tantobie to Blanchland, and was supervised by two Ministers. It was served by roads which at best were dirt tracks and at worst quagmires of mud. The sturdy independence of the Methodists has built up an enthusiastic community in which family loyalty plays a most important part.

St Mary's Roman Catholic Church, Blackhill

Until 1829, Roman Catholics had historically been denied many civil rights in England. However, the great reforms of the early nineteenth century saw the gradual emancipation of the Catholics.

As the Consett area became a hub of industrial activity, immigrant workmen from various parts of the British Isles made their way into the area looking for work. Many came from a somewhat less-than-friendly home in Ireland at that time, not least because of the Irish potato famines of the early and mid-1840s. The census returns of 1851 show that nearly 22 per cent of the immigrant workforce in Consett, and over 17 per cent of that in Blackhill was of Irish descent and native of Ireland. The rise in the number of Roman Catholics in the immigrant population of the time can perhaps best be indicated in part by the following;

Catholic Population in Brooms and Blackhill 1861-1882

Year	Brooms	Blackhill
1861	1134	2760
1874	2052	3220
1882	1800*	3600*

*approximate

Source: Status Animarum for the Diocese of Hexham and Newcastle Vol.2 (1847-1912)

It was realized at an early stage that further accommodation for Roman Catholics in the area would be necessary, as the nearest alternative place of worship was the Brooms Church near Leadgate. So it was in the early 1840s, when a tiny stone Roman Catholic Chapel was founded in Blackhill. Incidentally, the stone gable end of the present church hall facing Derwent Street in Blackhill is believed to be the last remaining piece of an earlier chapel, possibly the former property of the Primitive Methodists of the area.

The impetus for a new church was carried by a large proportion of the workmen employed under the Derwent Iron Company. The church was opened in 1857. Professing the Roman Catholic faith and desirous of a suitable building for services, they sought the help of Fr. Kearney of Brooms Church.

Mr Foster, the Manager of the ironworks, agreed to deduct funds from willing parishioners' wages. So successful was this scheme that the purchase of land and plans for buildings soon progressed. By 1854, steps were being taken to provide the local populace with a much more spacious place of worship.

The efforts of Fr. Kearney of Brooms who, it is thought, had figured among others in bringing peace and understanding to the community during the unrest of 1847, came to the fore again and he was instrumental in procuring the land on which the present St Mary's church at Blackhill now stands. As early as 1844, negotiations for land had been undertaken with Mr Hugh Brignall and Mr John Nicholson, who figured in the history of the area by finding iron ore on the 'blue heaps'.

The land in question bordered upon workers' cottages in Tin Mill Row built by a Mr. Bigge, believed to have been one of the original partners in the formation of the ironworks.

A little later, as designs were being drawn up for the new church, an indenture was made on 10 January 1855 between church dignitaries and Messrs. Brignall and Nicholson. Work gathered pace, although unfortunately a terrific hurricane demolished the almost complete building on 7 February 1856.

Undeterred, Fr. Kearney and the parishioners began again, and the building was completed and solemnly opened on the 24 July 1857 when the Pontifical High Mass was held by Bishop Hogarth, when it was given the official title of 'Our Blessed Lady Immaculate'.

The church which is situated in the heart of the town, on a site which commands an extensive view of the Derwent Valley, was of an entirely different and of much more substantial character and on a larger scale. It is by design, setting and beauty, a cathedral of completeness of arrangement, and is a very fine example, not only of early English architecture, but is also a reflection of the community's love of God by its dedication to the church.

It was to be many years before Consett town was itself able to boast any equal to the Blackhill structure.

(Reproduced with the kind permission of Mrs. Maureen Allen)

The Baptist Church, Highgate Corner, Blackhill

In the early years of the nineteenth century, Meeting Houses were built at Hamsterley in Weardale and at Cold Rowley (now Rowley). It was as a result of the enthusiasm and determination of the Rowley Pastor the Reverent E. le Fevre, who was Minister from 1851 until 1853, that a site for a church was obtained in 1851 at Highgate in Blackhill.

At this stage membership was restricted to baptised believers and the sacrament of the Lord's Supper was administered once a month to members only. Church discipline was very strict and exclusions were not uncommon. Evangelistic campaigns were regularly arranged and membership steadily increased as the church prospered. The faith and dedication of the community is seen in the finely appointed building in which prayer is held.

EMPLOYMENT OF YOUNG CHILDREN

As a result of the great Reform Bill of 1832, Royal Commissions to investigate the employment of young children were set up. In the following years, investigators recorded the extent of child employment, the working conditions and the general health and welfare of the children. Many industries were investigated, including in particular the heavy industries of mining and ironworks in the north of England.

Records of the Royal Commission at the time when the Derwent Iron Company was formed, show an appalling record of child employment in the north of England. Although there are no records of the early ironworks, there are records of the Bishopwearmouth ironworks, with which the Consett works was involved for some time. These records were used to gain a 'parallel' view of what working conditions may have been like for children in the early Derwent ironworks.

Generally, a child worker could be indentured or apprenticed from the age of fourteen. The older men in the ironworks would teach those who were indentured the skills of the trade. The man would pay the wage of about 4 shillings a week. This would rise about a 1 shilling per week each year, until the final two years, when they were given a 2 shillings a week increase. This scale applied to the works generally. Younger boys who worked in the forges and the mills were the servants of the proprietor, though paid by the men. The men were paid by the ton of wrought iron produced, the iron and coal being delivered to them by their employers. The men had to find the requisite labour, and so pay the boys when the wrought iron was produced. Proprietors would provide houses and fuel for the foremen and principal men, not for the others. The terms of payment for children were determined by custom of payment for particular work. The men understandably would take their own children in such cases, if the business was a good one; but proprietors would not allow children under ten to be employed in the Bishopwearmouth works. Here the men repaired the furnaces themselves on Sundays.

It was reported at the time by the Royal Commissioner investigating the ironworks that nothing more could be done by the masters for boys after they were actively engaged in the works, in the way of education. It was further felt that no certificate of education, as in the Factories Acts, could be enforced in an iron manufactory. Any compulsory enactments relating to education would be unneccessary, and not likely to be beneficial.

In an attempt to portray the working conditions of the time for young children, a random sample of five children from the Royal Commissioners' Report into the Employment of young children in the north of England is given below.

1) JOHN G ———

Aged 12 years old, he carries flats (flat bars of iron) to the warehouse. Cannot spell,read or write. Was learning his A, B and Cs at a day school, when he came away. Lives with his parents and sometimes goes to Sunday school or sometimes to Church.

2) ABRAHAM T———

Aged 10 years. Hooks up the iron that goes through the rolling mills. Comes to work at 5 o'clock a.m. and goes away at sometimes 6 or 7 at night. Gets 5s a week. Gets his meals when he has time. Cannot read, write or spell.

3) JOHN N———

Aged 14; is employed in faggoting, that is he collects together bits of iron, rings, keys and so on and binds them up in a bundle by two iron rings. Comes to work at 6 o'clock and leaves about 6 at night. His breakfast he brings with him, consisting of as much coffee and bread that he wants. He takes these at half-past eight a.m. having $1/2$ an hour allowed for that purpose. Generally he brings his dinner with him, consisting of 2 pennyworth of biscuits and coffee. Perhaps twice in a week his mother brings his dinner to him at the works, when it is generally bacon and baked potatoes. He does not leave work in general to take his breakfast or dinner. Gets his tea when he gets home of coffee and biscuits, very rarely any meat at all.

He works by piece work, getting 2s. 6d. per ton faggoted, and he generally faggots 5 tons in a fortnight. He is commonly employed in this work all the year around. Lives with his mother who does nothing for a living; gives her all his money. There are six of them in the family; two are sailors; two lasses are married, and the other bides in the house; is always pretty well in health. Cannot read, write or spell; never was at more than one school and has been away from that for four years. Was at that school for only two months, never goes to any Sunday School. A vast of the men swear; never heard of hell except when he heard men swearing about it. Mother does not teach him anything.

4) REDMAN L——

12 years of age; picks out scraps; gets sixpence a day. Lives with his parents, father is a chain maker. Cannot read, write or spell, left school about three years ago. Never goes to Sunday school or worship; has no clothes to go in. Plays about on Sundays. Hears the men swear a great deal. Never had any religious instruction; only his parents tell him not to swear.

5) THOMAS W——

Aged 16 years. Has been working for about seven years. When he first started at the age of nine, he drew the door of the furnace for six months; next trailed iron out at the forge for $2^1/_2$ years; worked then from twelve until twelve, in alternate three days night shift and three days day shift; next went to the rolling mills, lifting the iron up, from six until six, very often longer, if they were strong; sometimes until half past six or seven o'clock; never much later than seven o'clock. Next went to strike to the jobbing smith, at mending the tools for about a year. For two years was striking at the engine-smiths (the locomotive factory); then came to the forge about a year. Is now labouring in the yard in getting the iron ready for the furnaces. Now labours from six until six, sometimes until seven and gets 11 shillings for this. The longest hours worked was at the forge, generally from 4 a.m. until six at night, constantly. Was getting coals in and assisting the hammer-man. Some of the little boys are put upon sometimes; thinks they work too long hours. Can read fairly; can write his name; goes to school now; mostly goes to church or chapel.

The Child Coal and Ironstone Miners

Before the Royal Commissions were formed, children as young as three years old could be sent into the bowels of the earth. Because of the Reform Act of 1841, child labour below the age of ten years was forbidden. Children who worked usually did one of the following jobs:

TRAPPERS

The trapper's place of work was in the barrow way or roadway leading to the shaft of the pit. He would rise at 4 a.m. and be at the pit by 5 a.m. His job was to operate an air door, to open it when told by any of the drivers and to shut it after them. He had to remain at his place of work, or risk severe beatings from the drivers if they were held up, as they were on piecework. He would seat himself in a little hole about the size of a fireplace, and with a string in his hand, open and shut the door. Somtimes he had a candle for light, more often he sat in total darkness for up to twelve hours a day until told to leave his station at the end of the shift.

DRIVERS

When he was old enough, having gained strength and experience, the trapper would be promoted to driving a horse-drawn rolley from the coal face to the shaft bottom. This was piecework and they only got fed in their own time. It took many more long hard years of work before they could become putters or hewers.

LEADERS OF WATER AND WOOD

These were used to carry water or timber into the pit. Water was needed to keep the dust down or slake the thirst of the hewers and putters, and the wood to shore the sides and top of the roadway as progress was made into the coal face.

HELPERS

At other times they might become helpers up, when trams had become stuck or derailed, then a ready hand with strong back and perhaps a horse and limber to boot would solve the problem.

STONELEADERS

Stoneleaders were those boys who conducted carts of stone 'in-bye' (into the pit) for repairing the roads and sometimes for building walls of support along the sides of the roads.

From the information gleaned from the population census returns of 1851 for Consett and Blackhill, four children were found to be working in coal pits and a further three were working in ironstone mines. The ages of the children ranged from 10 to 14.

ENVIRONMENTAL HEALTH AND HOUSING

The health conditions of the first years of the town to follow the opening of the Derwent Iron Company are not known, although it is suggested that the early townspeople were little, if any, better off than those of any other industrial town of comparable size of the time. A great deal is owed to those pioneers of the years who campaigned long and hard for sanitary reform, especially in the new towns.

In 1842, Edwin Chadwick published his *Report on the Sanitary Conditions of the Labouring Populations*. The fact that this was in the years to follow the birth of ironmaking in the area shows the timeliness of his actions. The Report indicated (of Newcastle upon Tyne in particular) that eleven out of twelve houses had no running supply of water. It also revealed that, owing to unsanitary conditions nationwide, the number of deaths in one year from typhoid fever alone was double that of the number of lives lost by the allies at the Battle of Waterloo.

The difficulty lay in the facts of the situation. As the crowds of immigrant families poured into the new town, it seemed sufficient to subdivide houses to accomodate the extra people without consideration of the standard of the accommodation, especially when supply could not meet the demands on new housing. The occupied properties were made more insanitary and unhealthy by this influx of new labour. New arrivals therefore found themselves in housing which, though infinitely better than that they had endured before they came to Consett, still suffered from overcrowding, the lack of light, fresh air and a good supply of fresh water. The housing and health problem was not a new one, though the rapid increase and greater mobility of the population made it more serious.

It is quite possible that the difficulties with the local housing were an indirect result of the financial difficulties in which the Derwent Iron Company found itself in the 1850s.

Typical mid nineteenth-century housing at Consett.

In days when surgeons used to operate in filthy overalls, when the connection between dirt and infection was understood, but only dimly so, and without microscopes, then a tainted water supply was easily ignored. Perhaps in retrospect the most welcome gift to Victorian England was indeed the mass-produced drainpipes and water closets, and the political will to install them. At this time these were still, however, in their infancy.

However one may view history, there are individuals without whom change of any kind might well in retrospect not have taken place. Far-sighted men, many years before any statute was even thought of, considered those less fortunate than themselves and sought in some limited way to increase productivity by providing education for their young workers, and housing and security for the families who worked for them. The transition from the domestic 'cottage industry' to the factory system coincided with a whole series of measures to combat pauperism. The Quaker economist and social reformer John Bellers had published in 1696 'Proposals for raising the college of industry of all useful trades and husbandry with profits for the rich and plentiful living for the poor and a good education for youth'. This inspired the founding of many model villages and towns. Prominent among them were industrial villages such as Ambrose Crowley's Winlaton (1700) serving his large Durham hardware works.

Another Quaker in later years, Jonathan Richardson, entrepeneur, bank manager and proprietor of much land and mineral rights in the Consett area at the time, may well have been inspired by the work of others when he proposed and was in part responsible for building much of the early housing in Consett and Blackhill.

Extracts from the Parliamentary Commissioners' Reports, found in the Parliamentary papers of the state of the population in mining districts (1846) p.28-29, which deal with the early housing stock of Consett, can be found in Appendix III.

Such then, was the energy of the nineteenth-century entrepreneurs, in coal, iron, railways and other industries that they thought nothing of bringing camps, villages and even towns into existence in order to provide a labour force for their works. So it was that the north-west of Durham soon assumed the appearance of frontier camps on the edge of the Derwent valley. The houses and dwellings were of an extremely simple kind. However, it must be remembered that single-room dwellings were the norm until well into the twentieth century. The houses built when the Derwent Iron Company was formed were modern in the eyes of the builder and entirely functional. Economic and social mores of the time dictated that only the necessary was provided; to do any other was, in the eyes of the provider, a waste of money.

Houses at Puddlers Row, Consett Terrace, Blackleg Row and Pant Row, where the market and bus station exist today, would be thought of as being little more than hovels, with a single room up and down, a ladder to get from one room to the other, a stand-pipe for water, and an earthen privy. In some a small garden or allotment and a metalled road at the back were also provided. It was in these conditions that the early inhabitants of Consett worked and played and raised families.

It was in conditions such as these that in 1851, Ned Lennox was born. Of simple background, he became an engineer in the works. He must have had a natural aptitude toward music, for he taught the newly founded Consett Salvation Army Band to play the brass instruments which formed the first such brass band in all the world.

It may be of passing interest to observe how the population of Consett and Blackhill was affected in those early days by the growth of the industry. This can be seen in Appendices IV and V at the back of this book.

In 1811 the population was 139, in 1841, it numbered 195, and by 1851, when the works had been in operation for a little over ten years, the population had increased to 2228. Blackhill was still a wilderness. Gorse and whinny covered the area, stretching down towards the river Derwent and Shotley Bridge. Only a few houses would have been evident, perhaps Blackfyne House, Berry Edge cottage, now demolished, and a straggly array of simple dwellings following the sides of the Lanchester to Hexham turnpike road down past the Highgate to Shotley Bridge. There are, no doubt, still those in Consett and Blackhill today who can trace their ancestry through many generations to those who worked in the ironworks between its inception and the census return of 1851.

Despite the lack of records for the years 1841-1851, the Annual Reports of the Medical Officer of Health of Consett Local Board for the years 1896 and 1899 are of use in determining the likely environmental problems which the town suffered, and also the likely state of the town fifty years before. These reports are reproduced below in full.

Report of Medical Officer of Health 1896

There were outbreaks of measles, of whooping cough, scarlet fever and of enteric fever. Outbreaks were also reported of puerperal fever, erysipelas, diphtheria, influenza and membranous croup. In addition to the above, mortalities occurred as a result of diseases of the respiratory organs and typhoid fever.

BIRTHRATE/DEATHRATE IN CONSETT 1892-1899

	1892	1893	1894	1895	1896	1897	1898	1899
No. of Births	285	305	258	304	287	278	322	277
No. of Deaths	176	168	142	166	173	171	195	183
Birth rate	33.6	36.2	29.8	34.5	32.39	31.30	36.23	30.7
Death rate	20.8	19.8	16.4	18.8	19.52	19.24	22	20.3

Scarlet fever was reported on Albert Road, Boyd Street, Thomas Street, Pitt Street, Sherburn Terrace, Roseberry Terrace, Princes Street, Steel Street, the old Police Office, Puddlers Row, the new Railway Cottages and Forster Street. In this order - a total of 24 cases in all.

Diseases of the respiratory organs were common. The causes were blamed on the high exposed position of the district and the cold clay nature of the subsoil, on the faulty construction of a large number of houses, and on insanitary surroundings.

It was reported that in recent years a large number of houses of good construction and containing three or more rooms, have been erected in the district. In point of fact there were 71 in 1895 and 76 in 1896. They have all good through ventilation with the necessary out-offices. An objection which can be taken to many of them is that the sites are not made impervious over the whole area and therefore moisture and ground air have free access to the dwellers.

They all have fair sized yards but the chief objection is that they are not paved or cemented over the whole extent so that in wet weather water stands in them and causes a great deal of dirt to accumulate, besides rendering the foundations damp.

The older houses are of miserable construction and are quite out of date. The water supply is from the Consett Water Company reservoir on the Waskerley moors and is therefore free from source pollution. Notwithstanding the long drought of the summer, the supply has been fairly abundant and of good quality. The house drains with few exceptions are properly trapped; but the house drainage especially in the older tenements is not as it should be, the gully traps being close to the back doors and the adjacent grounds being either improved or only partially so.

The drainage of some of the streets is decidedly unsanitary, consisting of open brick channels, often defective, running at the backs of the dwellings and emptying themselves into large gullies, placed close to the habitations. The sewers are properly constructed pipe sewers with a good fall and are provided with ventilators. The sewerage is disposed of through three different channels. The main portion is carried direct to a considerable distance from the town and is spread over grassland without precipitation. The other portions find their way into the sewers of neighbouring districts.

EXCREMENT REMOVAL AND DISPOSAL

In connection with the older houses in the district the system for excrement disposal is the objectionable midden-privy. These erections are too close to the dwellings, are large, open, often below the level of the ground and do not provide for a proper admixture of excreta and ashes. There are also about 400 water closets in the town, but in many instances, they are filthy, very much neglected, and are very often rendered useless by the wanton destruction of the tenants. It would offer a salutory lesson, if a few of these offenders were prosecuted and made examples of.

The middens of the more modern dwellings are covered, ventilated and of late years, have assumed more reasonable dimensions. The cleaning of the ashpits and privies is performed by the Consett Iron Company in cases where the houses are their own property and the work is done fairly well. In the cases of private properties however, the tenants are expected to perform the work, and in consequence the ashpits are frequently overflowing and constitute a nuisance. I urge the Authority to undertake this work.

Report of Medical Officer of Health 1899

Several of the older dwellings have been improved. The upstairs rooms of the smaller 2 roomed cottages which have no fireplaces upstairs should have some kind of ventilator provided.

EXCREMENT AND DISPOSAL

A very large number of midden privies. The ash pits in many cases are much too large and uncovered with uncemented bottoms, and one ashpit frequently receives the excrement from three or four privies. There is no proper admixture of the excrement with ashes and often large pools of water, percolating through the basement can be found in the yards. Action taken to modify in short term and introduce water closets.

Many existing ashpit privies are surrounded by buildings constructed in the early history of the town and there is no means of access for the purpose of cleaning except through narrow passages which necessitate the filth being barrowed out onto the street before it reaches the scavenger's cart. The compulsory installation of water closets would no doubt mitigate this most disagreeable nuisance. Frequently observed that two or more lodgers in older two-roomed out-of-date cottages and the large number of single men principally engaged by the Consett Iron Company. To ask Consett Iron Company to make injunction of small cottages shall not keep lodgers and appoint their own House Inspector for the purpose.

In Nelson Street a one-roomed house above the urinal has been ordered to be closed and an order to restrict the number of inmates in the houses of the same yard which were overcrowded to be complied with.

Blue Row, Crookhall, front view, 10.9.24.

Blue Row, Crookhall, back view, 10.9.24.

General view showing demolition of Blue Row, Crookhall, 12.11.24.

Red Row, Crookhall.

THE TRUCK SYSTEM

Definition

'The partial or entire payment of wages in goods in the place of money.'

This method of payment was common in the early days of the factory system, when works were often situated some distance away from shopping centres. The supply of inferior goods and other abuses led to legislation (known as the Truck Acts) forbidding employers to lay down conditions as to the way workmen should dispose of their wages. Excuses given for running truck, or as they were otherwise known, Tommy shops, by the employers of the time, were that it was a service for which they had a right to be paid.

Contracts of employment also indicated that a worker should expect to have 'long pays', that is to be paid once a fortnight or even longer, perhaps monthly, depending upon the goodwill of the employer. The result of such payment was that the employees sometimes found that they had not sufficient money to last until the next payday, therefore were forced to ask the employer for credit in the truck shop.

Until the Statutes of the early 1870s mentioned above, there were no restrictions on how a man might be paid. If the master wished, he could pay in goods rather than in money. If the worker was lucky, and times were good and his job paid well, he would always have sufficient means to get him by to the next payday. This, however, was not always the case and examples have been drawn to illustrate the exploitation that the ordinary worker in the iron industry and indeed many others also, could suffer at the time. If there was a general depression in trading, then a worker's wage could be reduced to take account of the reduced profit that the master would have suffered as a result of the downturn of trading. In times of depression or low wages, anyone finding that he had not sufficient money to carry him through to the next pay day, could approach the truck shop for credit.

Because the prices were usually inflated, many a worker who had gained credit found that his master would not pay his wages, but kept the wages in payment of the truck that he had received. Many men were tied to the master's service as the master could give or withdraw credit as and when he wished to do so.

Sir David Dale, Managing Director of the Consett Iron Company, gave evidence in the Truck Act Enquiry of 1871. This indicated that there had been a truck shop in the ironworks at Consett, although this had gone out of business some time earlier because of the formation of a Co-operative wholesale shop in the area during the 1840s.

Statement of Sir David Dale, Managing Director of Consett Iron Company, examined before the Royal Commission on the Truck System on the 26th January 1871.

Present Mr. Bowen.   *Examined Sir David Dale.*
Quoting Sir David Dale:

I am the Managing Director of Consett Iron Company, we have about 4,000 men. Our works are collieries, blast furnaces and rolling mills, and rail and plate making.

All of our establishments are paid fortnightly, except the forges and the rolling mills, where there are 2,000 hands. They have a weekly intermediate payment calculated as nearly as may be within 5 per cent of the amount earned.

There is no difficulty whatever in arriving at a computation weekly in the case of the rolling mills or the forges. The men are quite satisfied with the estimates we give.

Weekly pays would undoubtedly entail a considerable inconvenience; still it would be a question whether that inconvenience ought not to be faced. The competition of towns prevents the evils of long pays.

With regard to the benefit which a Truck Master derives from that system it is impossible to speak with perfect exactness, because it depends upon the completeness of his system; but roughly, I think that the iron manufacturer who keeps a complete truck shop has his wages 10 per cent lower than his neighbours, that being the profit that he derives from operating the truck shop.

If a comparison was instituted between Wales and the north of England, they being the great rail competing districts, it would be found that first that the profit actually derived by the Welsh Masters who keep Truck shops is an aid to their legitimate profits; and next, that the long prevalence of Truck has had a material influence in enabling them to maintain their competition with the north of England, by the general subservience which it has produced in the people.

Not only to the extent that the truck system does prevail at any ironworks in Wales; as the keeper of a truck shop who is also an iron manufacturer benefited to the extent of something like 10 per cent on his wages as compared with the north of England, being the profit that he derives from keeping the truck shop.

But also there is found to exist throughout those districts where the Truck system prevails, an absence of the freedom and independance which is found amongst the men in the north of England, and the consequence of that is, a generally lower prevailing rate of wages.

There is no truck in the north of England in connection with collieries and iron mines or ironworks. It did exist, but it has been quite abandoned. Co-operative stores are spreading very generally. There is one in connexion with the Consett Ironworks which has 600 members and in which the expenditure in goods and wages is about £24,000 annually.

I would say that roughly if the average earnings of the truck master were 26 shillings a week and the Truck shop was a very complete concern including articles of clothing as well as articles of food, and if the wages were long so as to drive most of the men into the Truck shop, it would not be unfair to assume that at least 16 shillings a week of each mans earnings was spent in the Truck shop and the profit on that 16 shillings would not be less than 3 shillings, which upon the wages and earnings of the men would represent something like more than $12^1/_2$ per cent.

No capital would be needed for the truck shop as the goods would be paid for by a two or three months bill.

I say that the keeper of a truck shop getting those three months credit upon the 16s spent per man per week, is really raising a capital of £10 per man.

Of course I am putting that as an extreme case, where the truck shop is complete and the wages long and drive every man to use it.

I do not suppose that anything of this kind is found; but it is quite possible to work the system to that extent, and I have no doubt that there are isolated cases in which it does occur. I should think that at any rate a modified truck system would create the capital to the extent of £5 per man.

The shop would represent the creation rather than the absorption of capital.

Whether the assistance of a Truck shop would help to float a company in a time of depression would depend very much on the tenure of the works.

In the north of England the establishments are all very large and are not held on lease.

In other parts of England and Wales they are generally rented, and a much smaller capital is required.

WITH REFERENCE TO THE ARGUMENT AS TO THE EFFECT OF SHORT PAYS UPON DRINKING

I do not think that it is for an employer to say 'I will not pay frequently, because I believe the man will drink'.

My feeling is that one must assume that either the man's habits are, or will become those of self respect and self restraint, and we should pay them as if they were so.

The leaders of the men's union in the north of England are almost all teetotallers, and that upon which they would chiefly dwell in their communications with the men would be the importance of abstaining from drink if they wish to hold their own in the competition with capital.

In the collieries we simply have fortnightly pays without draws. It would not be possible to have weekly pays there, because of the distances of the collieries. I think it would be hardly possible without a very considerable increase in the staff.

A great deal of their shopping is done in the large towns to which they have train facilities for going.

The statement continued for some six pages of typescript in total, from which the above are extracts.

Evidence of 'Truck' in the Nail Trade

WESTWOOD S.
I am a nailmaker. There are many 'foggers' (middle men) in the district. The men are expected to go to the shop. If they do not they are slighted in every way. They do not get work. I have known men to sell goods to get money. I have had flour offered to me; cheese, butter, bacon and sugar are also sold. That is, when people want money in the middle of the week. I have never heard of tobacco being sold. The system of 'foggers' is more severe now (1871) than it ever was. I remember when the Truck Act was passed (the first Truck Act was passed in 1831). Before that the people used to have notes for the warehouse to go down to the warehouse for their goods, but afterwards the fogger had to pay the money in the warehouse. I was a boy at the time, and after three or four men had been paid I had to go down to the shop and bring up the cash to pay the hands with. The Act did some good, but it did not last long. There are plenty of men who would come forward to give evidence, but they are afraid to do so.

PARTRIDGE J.
I am a nailmaker. I have worked for Thomas P–. I was expected to take the greatest part of my wages in provisions. He has spoken to me about it frequently. He said to me 'How many children have you?' He has then said to me 'Well, you do not spend enough money and if you do not spend more money, of course, you cannot look to me for work'. The articles in his shop were very inferior. The flour was not fit for a pig to eat. It was 8d dearer than elsewhere.

I worked for a Samuel P–. He had a shop and a beerhouse. I was always paid in cash there, but I was expected to go to the shop. I was not told so, but I knew from experience that if I did not I would have no work. He would bring in his book into the beerhouse and ask the men how much they had had in the shop, and was the same system there. We were expected to go to the shop and if we did not we did not get any money.

There is a great deal of distress. Most men's homes were ridiculous to look at; there was only one room for seven grown grown-up people to sleep in. When I worked for P– I have bought goods from the shop and sold them at a reduction to make up my rent.

SIVITER T.

I am a nailmaker. I have seen the system as it has been worked, although I have not worked for a fogger for 14 years. When I worked for a fogger he kept a beerhouse and a Tommy shop. We had to go on the Monday morning for orders, and perhaps they would say that they had none for us. Then we would go back again on Tuesday, but there would still be no orders. The same thing would be done on the Wednesday and the Thursday morning before there was any orders given to us.

The object was to keep us under their thumb. Sometimes they had not gotten the iron they could have gotten, if they had liked. I could get beer on credit, the tendency of the trade has been to convert ready money paying masters from employers of labour into employers of foggers, because otherwise they are undersold by the market foggers. I think the prices and qualities are not the same as those in ordinary shops. Some have the quality, but charge a higher price; others have not the quality, and charge the same price.

My average wages will be about 12 shillings a week. That would be above the average of men. Nailers wages are often mistaken when compared with those of other labourers, because they have charges to pay. Sometimes foggers will give us iron which does not suit the work, and then the man has to go to an iron changer in order to get the proper iron, and we have to pay 1d or 2d a bundle for the iron being changed. The fogger has himself got some relation who is an iron changer. I have to pay 1d for getting the iron, and then to carry it all about the place to find some that will suit me, and then pay another penny for changing it. I have to supply myself out of my wages with my rent, and the rent and the coals for my smithy.

I think about 14,000 out of 24,000 nailmakers are trucked. At certain times I have been deprived of work, because the ready money master for whom I was working did not just at that time have any orders. Then when his orders came in he would have to resort to petty foggers because they would have the nails by them. There is a great deal of poverty in the district, much more than there seems to be. It is principally among those who work to the foggers, they are the poorer class of workmen.

And so the testimony went on. Thankfully the 1871 Truck Acts put an end to almost two centuries of worker exploitation in this way, by ensuring the payment of wages in the coin of the realm.

EARLY SOCIAL DISTURBANCES OF THE AREA

Of all the factors of production, none is as important to industry as labour. The labour force of any population may be of the same or different backgrounds, cultures and upbringing. Whether or not these ethnic groups keep separate from other groups, or freely intermingle, the prime function of the individual within any of the groups is to work and make a living to serve the community in which he or she lives.

As has been already stated, the area of Consett was thinly populated in 1840, with Shotley Bridge being the nearest settlement of any consequence. It was said that by 1858 there were about 20 000 people in the vicinity of Consett, most of whom were either directly or indirectly dependant upon the operations of the ironworks. The influx of new workers of diverse origin became an essential part of the lifeblood of the infant town of Consett. Their skills both added to the quality and diversity of product, and they forged an understanding of differing culture and belief that aided a tolerant community that exists even today.

At an early stage in the development of the ironworks the considerable immigration of labour had caused no small amount of aggravation. This is recorded in history in the fact that the immigrants seem to have broken into two national groups and, related to nationalities, into two religious groups. On the one hand there were the English, predominantly Protestant, and on the other the Irish, of whom the majority were Roman Catholic. These at first created social problems for which there were no obvious solutions. For many years the Irish and indigenous populations of the town both kept themselves segregated in all except work.

This religious difference gave rise to a whole series of open conflicts during the 1840s, culminating in that most legendary of clashes in November 1847, remembered and still spoken of as the Battle of the Blue Heaps. It was said that such disturbances were caused by drink and religious antagonism and were not uncommon during the formative days of the new community at Consett.

The fact that those antagonisms of November 1847 were never repeated suggests that those caught up in them were in the main responding superficially to religious antagonisms, and that the real cause could well have been any one of the hundreds of events taking place during the formative years of the new and vibrant society of a wild and near lawless frontier town in which they lived and were a part of. As a spectator of history (as we all are) efforts were made to find out whatever was possible about the disturbances, and to ask the question, how will history judge the events written about here?

The following is an account of information gleaned from newspapers of the day and of public records, and shows a different light on the happenings at the 'Riots of the Blue Heaps'.

One may see the enlightened manner with which the matter was dealt with by the courts. None of those charged with rioting were gaoled for the offence, but were each bound over to keep the Queen's peace for a period of one year for the sum of £20 each. Of the 195 men sent for trial at the Quarter Sessions that dealt with the twelve men, only those same twelve were bound over to keep the peace. Neither was there anything found to suppose that any of those charged ever broke their bond, or indeed any other law again, rather that they just faded into history.

Indeed, one individual can be recognized from the census returns of 1851, perhaps as having been a headstrong young man of 22 years at the time of being brought to the Quarter Sessions in 1848, to reappear in the society of 1851 Consett as a skilled and responsible citizen having settled down to work and raising a family.

Soldiers were brought in to restore order but this was nothing exceptional under the circumstances, as their function was, in part, to assist the civil police as requested. The area was 'under-policed', although this again was no-one's fault in particular, because the authorities themselves seem to have been overtaken by the events of the Industrial Revolution and the birth of new towns in much the same way as in other parts of the country. The overall picture suggested that there were great numbers of disowned land workers or immigrant labour roaming the country seeking work and shelter. Homeless, hungry and almost penniless, needing to find warmth and security, many came to areas like Consett where there was a likelihood of finding work.

The ordinary citizen, whether immigrant or native, had little right of redress under any circumstance, to the hopelessness of his situation. The ordinary man had no right to vote. He had no one to turn to for help, other than to those who shared his predicament. Families already in work or housing could easily be frightened into believing that anyone other than those they knew personally could be seeking to take their hard-earned security from them.

Eighteenth- and nineteenth-century history has shown many times that riot was the valve by which society gave vent to any pent up anger or frustration. It was in part for these very reasons that the Riot Act of 1715 was entered upon the statute books. In 1847-48 riots were also taking place in Newcastle, Gateshead and Sunderland and along the north east coast of England for a variety of reasons.

The disturbances can in retrospect be seen as an act of desperation caused by a feeling of hopelessness in those concerned, not only because of religious differences (which admittedly did exist to some small degree), but rather because of the social, economic and industrial conditions of the day.

The Riot Act

The purpose of the Riot Act of 1715 was to give strengthened powers to Local Authorities to apprehend rioters, once they had been duly warned to disperse, so that they might be prosecuted as felons. Even more important was the fact that the law enforcers were indemnified should any rioters be hurt or killed; whereas under the common law it was possible to prosecute them for anything from assault to murder. When a body of men were 'riotously or tumultously assembled together', a magistrate came as near as he safely dare and read to them, in the name of the Queen, a proclamation ordering the rioters to disperse. But even the reading of the Riot Act could not take place within a hour of the riot starting and, because of this, much damage could be caused in that time. The Riot Act was the main statutory weapon of the scattered, amateur enforcement officers who (with the final resort to soldiers) bore the responsibility for keeping England peaceful until even after the establishment of a professional police force in the nineteenth century.

Who would try them?

The felons were tried by Justices of the Peace, usually appointed by the Crown and on the advice of the Lord Lieutenant of the county. The choice was usually from the most worthy and respectable gentlemen of the county, gentry and the clergy. They were not trained in the law, unless they happened to be landowners who had had to train in law in their own right. They were advised upon the legal questions by the Clerk of the Peace, which was usually combined as a purely formal office with that of the Lord Lieutenant. Brought before the court for summary jurisdiction, the facts of the case would be examined, often in a house of the Justice of the Peace.

The Justice of the Peace had to make a preliminary investigation to decide whether the accused should be sent to trial and come to a decision.

The Quarter Sessions

The principal court of the Justices was the Quarter Sessions, held in each county four times a year and attended by all the Justices of that county. The Quarter Sessions was a full Criminal Court, with a jury theoretically capable of trying any case short of treason, although by custom all serious cases were sent to the assizes.

The following are extracts from personal diaries made at the time, for which many thanks are offered to the Consett Lions for their kind permission to reproduce them from the book, *The Consett Story*.

CONSETT IN 1844 BY MR JOHN CALVERT

In passing the Highgate public house I witnessed a sight which was not uncommon in those days. In the lower rooms of the public house there was not a table or a chair but had its legs broken off, and these a number of mad, drunken fellows were wielding to some purpose on each others' heads.

The landlord, a Mr Moore, was in his shirt sleeves, and his arms from his hands to his elbows were just as though he had dipped them in blood. I have stood in my own doorway and counted a dozen fights all going on at the same time. The road in front of my house was, in winter, knee deep in mud and in many places a horse was in danger of disappearing altogether.

EXTRACT OF 8 FEBRUARY 1846

By far the most serious encounter took place at Moore's house where a party of English and Irish workmen met. An Irishman having been seriously beaten, his countrymen armed themselves with sticks, stones and other missiles, and commenced an attack on the house by smashing the window. Soon after the English were joined by a number of their comrades when a desperate encounter ensued, which lasted several hours, during which forty or fifty on each side were more or less disabled by cuts and bruises. The riot continued until 2 o'clock the following morning, and it was necessary to call out a large body of policemen to restore order. Three of the more seriously injured subsequently died of their wounds.

EXTRACT OF 1847 BY JOHN MEWES (believed to be a grocer from Blackhill at the time)

I have not seen much excitement but I shall never forget the Berryedge riot though it was a canny bit ago. I well remember the day upon which it broke out. It was I believe on a Sunday and I was out with another tradesman when he suggested that we should go into a public house for a slight refresher. However, when we had not long been there when we heard an angry and excited clamour of voices. Immediately afterward a gang of men rushed into the place and we hurried out of it as sharply as we could.

When I reached home I found the shutters up and the windows barred with the doors securely fastened. I tapped at the shutters and fortunately for me my wife guessed who it was and at once admitted me.

But I was glad to get into safer quarters, for the men outside were mad with passion, and were swearing a terrible vengeance. The soldiers were brought over, and they remained till the riot was quelled. I am certain the riot lasted three days, and I believe four. Some people actually went to the country to their friends.

THE BATTLE OF THE BLUE HEAPS
(FROM THE CONSETT STORY)

The different memories as to how this trouble actually originated are somewhat vague, but racial animosity (now happily practically extinct in the district), combined with sundry trade jealousies in stirring up a feud which at one time seemed about to break out into a very serious riot. One side held possession of the mounds between Consett and Blackfyne, which are known by the fanciful title mentioned above. They were, in the main, Irish newcomers into the neighbourhood, whose coming, rightly or wrongly, was resented by those who were already engaged in the place as workers.

The occupants of the blue heaps were amply supplied with ammunition in the shape of stones, and armed with rude weapons of offence. They might even pride themselves on possessing an artillery train, for a small cannon, intended for saluting purposes, had been commandeered into service, and was mounted to decimate the ranks of the attacking parties. Luckily for the latter, (and possibly even for the safety of the occupying garrison) this weapon was never fired.

The disturbances and particularly the rumours of intended strife were, however, so prevalent and alarming that military aid was hastily summoned, and the next day saw a company of soldiers quartered in Shotley Bridge to guard against any possible contingency.

Meanwhile influential gentlemen known well to each of the belligerents, worked most earnestly to bring affairs to a peaceful conclusion. Among these a name that is always mentioned with high praise was the former Roman Catholic priest of Leadgate, Canon Kearney, whose advice and powers of persuasion had a most beneficial effect.

BLACKHILL AT THE TIME OF THE RIOTING
(FROM THE CONSETT STORY)

The low roofed houses at the top of Blackfyne were in existence, but only a straggly array of houses marked the progress of Durham Road down to Cutlers Hall Road. West Row, then in its palmy days, looked out as it does now over the Derwent valley. It went under the name of Old Blackhill to distinguish it from its later rival, Derwent Street which was known as New Blackhill.

Houses were springing up rapidly in rows between the two and so great was the demand for work in those days that these houses were frequently occupied by families while yet so necessary a part as the roof was still wanting. These houses were run up with no regard to appearance and little to convenience, as the region known as Bottle Bank exemplifies.

The neat comfortable houses of the company rows from Laburnum Avenue to Bessemer Street were as yet unthought of. Cemetery Road was an unkempt footpath, dangerous to travel after nightfall, and a scattered plantation of trees covered most of the site. A gloomy and barren waste extended from this point up to the township of Consett, covered with scant herbage and usually impassable because of the mire. No one who saw the wildernesss at that period would ever have thought that it would blossom like a rose, but it was this unpromising tract which has since become, under the auspices of the former Consett Iron Company, the elegant and trimly kept park of the district.

EXTRACT FROM THE QUARTER SESSION RECORD QS/O/26, DURHAM COUNTY COUNCIL ARCHIVE RECORDS, 3 JANUARY 1848:

Durham at Quarter Sessions of the Peace of our Lady. Before Roland Burdon, John Fogg Elliot and Anthony Wilkinson esq., and their fellow justices and also to hear and determine divers felonies, trespass and other misdeameanours done and said in the said county.

'The prisoners having pleaded guilty to an indictment of riot at the Parish of Lanchester, it is ordered that they severally enter into cognisance to keep the peace for twelve calendar months or otherwise to be brought up to abide the judgement of the court. And thereupon, the said:

1   Henry Jackson
2   Heron Lowe
3   Henry Smiles
4   Thomas Kearton
5   Hugh McCoglin
6   Smith Pearson
7   John Davison
8   Joseph Milburn
9   James Murphy
10   Patrick Lawson
11   John FitzPatrick and
12   John McAvay

acknowledge themselves to owe to our Sovereign Lady the sum of £20 each, to be levied upon their goods and chattels, lands and tenements.

To the use of our said Lady the Queen, her Heirs and successors upon failure of performing the following condition, that is to say, upon the condition that the said twelve (indicted) severally do keep the peace and be of good behaviour toward our said Lady the Queen and all her liege subjects for the space of twelve calendar months then this recognisance to be void or otherwise to remain in full force.

It would be interesting to know what sort of men were these brought before the courts on such a serious charge. Certainly there was no record of any of the twelve men ever having been brought up to a court during the following twelve months and so they never broke their bond.

A further examination of the same record in County Hall also gives Quarterly Reports from the Chief Constable of County Durham, and of the Governor of Durham Gaol. The following are but three small extracts of record, one from each of the above gentlemen, and a random extract which could give some small indication as to the social conditions, not only in the Consett area, but in many other parts of the county.

EXTRACT FROM REPORT OF DURHAM COUNTY CHIEF CONSTABLE, MAJOR JAMES WEMYSS, TO THE WINTER SESSION 1847-1848

It appears neccessary you should be apprised that for a considerable time past I have been receiving applications for policemen from various parts of the county and that from the limited number of the force there has been no means of affording the protection required by that increase in the population, that increase being of an unruly description in some localities. According to the census of 1841, those parts of the county which are rated for the maintenance of the Constabulary force contained a population of 206,449, which no doubt has greatly increased during the last seven years by the extension of coal and ironworks etc.

To superintend this population there are 90 policemen so that if the proportion of policemen by the Act were as one to two thousand, there would still be 13 policemen required to complete that amount. But the Act gives Magistrates the power of appointing one constable for every one thousand of the population - as at present established each constable has the charge of 2,293 supposing there had been no increase in the population since the last census.

At Shotley Bridge Ironworks, a population not of the most orderly habits amounting to some 18,000 has sprung up within a few years and an increase in the police force in this district is imperatively called for, there being at present only two officers stationed in that vicinity. The necessity of additional protection there has been manifested by the rioting which has recently occurred as well as on former occasions and by the fact of the company keeping three or four private policemen at their own expense.

There have been applications from Sacriston and Edmondsley, Willington and Medomsley and Hylton or West Boldon; also from Blaydon which last has been supplied by withdrawing a man from Hylton. These applications are made for your consideration.

EXTRACT FROM REPORT OF THE GOVERNOR OF DURHAM GAOL TO THE WINTER SESSION 1847-1848.

Result of Cases Sent to Trial

	sent to		
	Assizes	Sessions	Total
Executed	1		1
Transported	24	11	35
Imprisoned	59	123	182
Not Guilty	20	34	54
No Bills ?	6	3	9
No Prosecution	3	4	7
To be discharged at the rising of Court	1	-	1
Did Not Appear	1	-	1
Bound over to keep the peace for 12 months		12	12
Indictments quashed	-	2	2
Postponed to Assizes		6	6
	115	195	310

There were a total number of cases of 2083 for the year of which only 77 came from the parish of Lanchester in which Consett was situated. Of the total, 84 were smiths and foundrymen and 35 were either glassblowers or puddlers.

RANDOM EXTRACT OF QUARTER SESSION RECORD QS/O/26

Removal of Scotch and Irish Poor

It is ordered that the County Treasurer do pay unto Henry Burdon Taylor of Sunderland in the County of Durham Relieving Officer, the sum of £18. 15s. 5d being the costs incurred by him in the removal of Scotch and Irish Poor from the Parish of Sunderland near the sea, in the said County, Pursuant to the Act 8th and 9th Victoria cap.117 June 1848.

REPORT OF THE VISITING JUSTICES OF THE DURHAM GAOL AND HOUSE OF CORRECTION TO THE WINTER SESSIONS 1847-1848.

The number of prisoners committed to the gaol and house of correction during the past three months has been unusually large, showing an excess over the corresponding period of the proceeding year of 162; an addition of nearly one third.

This excess is chiefly attributable to the cessation or contraction of manufacturing operations and railway works, consequent upon the state of the money market together with an extensive emigration to this county of paupers from Ireland; causing our roads and streets to be beset with the families of labourers who have been cast adrift and with mendicants in search of the means of subsistence. A large number of summary convictions and committals for petty theft is the inevitable consequence of this unusual migration. In this class of commitments, the typhus fever has on different occasions been introduced into the prison but we have the satisfaction of stating that the precautions taken were sufficient to prevent the spread of fever and with the exception of one individual (a temporary officer engaged to attend upon the fever patients, who we cannot say caught the disease and died of it) infection has not been conveyed to any inmate of the prison, and at this instant we are entirely free from typhus.

There are three male prisoners in a precarious state of health from pulmonary affection. The above are the exceptions to the generally healthy state of the prisoners; and the exception from greater sickness in the gaol during the prevalence of so much illness around is strong testimony to the cleanliness and good ventilation of the buildings and to the perfect compatibility of the discipline and restraint of the separate system of imprisonment with the preservation of health.

Several weeks elapsed after the last sessions before the health of Mr Hopton would allow us to seek an explanation of the great excess in the consumption of provisions while he was storekeeper and compared with the subsequent period, but after hearing what Mr Hopton had to say when he acknowledged to having entrusted the key of the provision stores to prisoners we informed him of our intention to fill up his situation. There has been no appointment however owing to the short space of time since our interview with him and to offer causes unconnected with Mr Hopton.

Now that the price of labour is reduced the Bench will perhaps deem it expedient to proceed with the enlargement of the prison for females and the conversion of such portions of the old criminal prison as is practicable to cells suitable for the separate system.

John Elliot
W L Wharton

Further evidence of the happenings of those early years at Consett and Blackhill are to be found in a variety of other sources, including the newspapers of the day which are on record in the Local History section of any County Library.

Reported on the morning of the 26 November 1847 in the Durham Advertiser of a happening at Blackhill near Shotley Bridge 12 days earlier on the 14 November 1847.

RIOT IN BLACKHILL

Eleven out of the twelve persons have been apprehended as ringleaders in a serious affray which occurred in the above neighbourhood on the 14 inst., between the English and Irish workmen employed by the Derwent Iron Co., and on Friday last were committed by the Magistrates at Shotley Bridge to take their trial at the ensuing Quarter Sessions on the charge of riot, and Mr Smith of this city (Durham) has been retained as solicitor to conduct the prosecution.

The committal of these persons appears to have had good effect, as the district has since been in a state of comparative quietude, although it was reported that the English workmen had meditated an attack upon the Roman Catholic Chapel situated in that neighbourhood either on Saturday or Sunday evening last.

This however, did not take place, arising probably from the fact of a detachment of the county police having been promptly stationed in that locality. The conduct of the police during the recent excitement in this part of the county has been highly praiseworthy.

The following is an extract from the Newcastle Journal, 20 November 1847

Riot at Conside ironworks - some disturbance took place on Sunday at Conside ironworks near Shotley Bridge in County Durham. In consequence of serious disputes between the Irish and English labourers employed there, which have been aggravated by large numbers of the unemployed parties having come there from other places in the expectation of getting work in which they were disappointed. There had been previously a quarrel between the parties and some skirmishing in which the English were victors; and on Sunday the Irish mustered strong, with the intention of revenging their past injuries.

The tumult at one time rose to a great height, stones were thrown and in one case a knife was drawn, but happily the Manager of the works with great firmness and energy, interfered and expostulated with the men on their impropriety of their conduct with such good effect that order was eventually restored, but not until severe injuries had been inflicted on both sides. Several of the ringleaders being known were subsequently taken into custody and after undergoing examinations before the magistrates on Tuesday, were committed for various terms of imprisonment.

Several others known to have taken part in the affray have since been apprehended and were yesterday examined before the Magistrates at Shotley Bridge. Great complaints are made of the want of an efficient police. The Durham rural establishment seems to be of no use whatever in that quarter, notwithstanding the heavy expense which it entails upon the county.

Later, in the same newspaper of 8 January 1848 it was reported:

Durham Quarter sessions, the General Quarter Sessions of the Peace for the County of Durham commenced on Monday past, before Rowland Burdon esq., and a bench of Magistrates and were closed on Tuesday. The number of prisoners confined in the gaol and House of Correction in 1847 far exceeded that of those confined in 1846. In the former year the number was 257 and latter 178. The trials were of little interest.

EPILOGUE
Consett: Twelve Years On

For 140 years Consett had been the classic company town. 'The Works' and 'The Company' dominated the place both economically and socially. Consett's prosperity and social life were inextricably linked to steel. Sons followed fathers into the steelworks. The Works, visible on the skyline for miles around, physically dominated Consett - huge structures belching smoke and spreading the famous red dust. All that is now history.

THE CLOSURE

In December 1979 the British Steel Corporation (BSC) announced its intention to close Consett Works. Already the Hownsgill Place Mill had been shut down two months before and employment was also falling through rationalisation measures - which, BSC had said, would help keep the works viable. BSC, in the throes of financial crisis brought about by over-expansion, deepening recession and pressure from the new Conservative government, was desperate to cut capacity. Consett was an obvious target - isolated, small, marginal - and was to become an early victim of a massive programme to rationalise smaller steel plants right across the country. In these circumstances, Consett did not have much of a chance of reversing the decision.

The trade unions mounted a 'Save Consett' campaign, with lobbying, marches, rallies and the presentation of a petition at Downing Street. Campaigners argued - correctly - that the plant was profitable and could have a future as a quality producer. But BSC's concern was, quite simply, to cut capacity. Eventually, the unions were forced to accept defeat and negotiate severance terms. On 12 September 1980, the final batch of steel was produced. Attempts by a 'mystery consortium' to buy the plant ended in acrimonious failure and the furnaces were finally blown out in late September. Consett's 140-year history of iron and and steel-making had decisively ended.

The decision to close the steelworks brought much anger and bitterness, coupled with real fears for the future. There was talk of Consett becoming a ghost town, the 'Jarrow of the 1980s'. Some people had been resigned to the closure; it came as a shock but was not totally unexpected - the possibility had been rumoured for years. And a few were pleased to have the chance to leave the harsh conditions of the works and saw the redundancy pay-off as an opportunity to start a new life. But for everyone involved it was a massive upheaval that had a major impact on their lives. Not surprisingly, it is still talked about in Consett and the causes and consequences continue to be debated; it is often regarded as a watershed, separating two eras: before and after The Closure.

To what extent has Consett recovered over the years since the closure? Certainly in Consett itself there is no consensus on this but many conflicting views and interpretations. Some argue that a great transformation has been achieved, with the creation of a new and modern economic base and a better environment. Others say that the new economy is made up of 'fly-by-night' firms offering 'Mickey Mouse' jobs and feel that Consett might never recover. The media, still fascinated by the place, has variously portrayed Consett as an industrial graveyard, a no-hope town sacrificed on the altar of Thatcherism or, increasingly these days, a phoenix risen from the ashes. Sensationalism and cliche abound: exemplified perhaps by the television documentary of the early 80s titled 'Town for Sale' and, by contrast, a more recent Daily Mail story headlined 'Doomed Steel Town is Booming Again'. The truth lies, as ever, somewhere between these extremes and is inevitably much more complex.

IMPACTS

Back in the early 1980s, the outlook was, undoubtedly, very grim. The closure of the steelworks, making 3700 redundant, had made the local unemployment problem, already serious, very much worse. On top of this came yet more local job losses as nearby branch factories (notably Ransome, Hoffman, and Pollard at Tanfield Lea) shut down or drastically cut their workforces. Between mid-1980 and mid-1981 half of Derwentside's manufacturing jobs disappeared and the district's unemployment rate doubled to 27 per cent by July 1981. By the end of 1981, a third of Derwentside's men were on the dole. Younger ex-steelworkers wondered whether they would ever work again; those in their fifties became convinced that their working lives were over. In the early 1980s it looked as if Consett might slide into terminal decline, a sort of enormous, decaying 'Category D' village.

POLICIES

At the time of the steelworks closure it was clearly recognised that there was a vital need to bring new jobs to the area. It was obvious, too, that this was going to be an uphill struggle since Consett had so little to offer apart from unemployed labour. Since no-one was prepared for this disaster - even though it was not wholly unexpected - Consett had little serviced industrial land or factories to rent to new firms. It was also isolated, ill-served by road communications and environmentally despoiled. All these deficiencies had to be remedied to give Consett a chance.

In the wake of the closure, a 'task force' was formed, bringing together key instituitions of central and local government to implement a strategy to aid the area's recovery. The plan involved four interrelated elements: major investment in a new road link from Consett to the A1 motorway; the provision of factory premises; reclamation of the steelworks site; and the use of subsidies and other assistance to establish new industry.

Gradually, these policies have been implemented and they have, without doubt, had an impact. The new road link has been built and a substantial new industrial estate, Consett Number One, has been established. To many, the most obvious and striking result has been the removal of the steelworks, involving a massive ten-year reclamation project. Today, there is a vast grassy site, 700 acres of emptiness, where the works once stood, and evidence of Consett's industrial past is difficult to find. But the key part of the strategy, to 're-industrialise' Consett, has been the most difficult to achieve and its impacts are the most contentious, with unresolved arguments about the numbers and types of jobs created.

ECONOMIC DEVELOPMENT

The re-industrialisation effort was initially started by BSC (Industry) Ltd, the 'social conscience' subsidiary of BSC, which set up in Consett in 1979 and which later spawned the Derwentside Industrial Development Agency. The agency's role is to help small businesses become established, to encourage industry to move to the area and to support the expansion of existing companies. The agency and Derwentside Council are able to give advice and guidance but, above all, to help secure subsidies from central and local government, BSC (Industry), the European Community and venture capital companies. Businesses setting up in Consett have been able to get an impressive range of grants and loans and quite a number have come to take advantage of what is claimed to be one of the best incentive packages in Europe.

In the first few years after the closure progress was slow. While some new jobs were created, they were offset by continued job losses in the rest of the economy. At that time, officials privately admitted that the best they could manage was 'to run fast to stay in the same place'. Unemployment remained very high in the first half of the 1980s and only really started to subside significantly in the second half of the decade as national economic recovery reached the North East. For many in Consett, the best prospect to be found at the Job Centre (locally dubbed the 'Joke Shop') was a place on a government scheme.

Slowly, however, a new economic base has been established and there has been a degree of recovery in Consett in the last five years or so. The subsidies, together with investment in roads and environmental improvements, have helped bring new jobs in a diverse range of industries. About 1200 people now work in factories on the Number One estate - where ten years ago there were fields - and local development agencies claim that 5000 new jobs have been created in the firms they have helped in Derwentside. Consett, once famous for steel, is now known for Phileas Fogg snack foods - a truly remarkable transformation.

Unemployment fell significantly during the second half of the 1980s - by March 1990 the number of people out of work and claiming benefit in Derwentside was down to 3418 as compared with 7208 in September 1986. Part of this was due to statistical changes, to people finding work outside the area and to the fact that older ex-steelworkers left the employment register on reaching 60. But there is no doubt that a considerable number of new jobs have been created and this contributed to the shortening of Consett's dole queues. Sadly, the current recession has reversed this trend, bringing increasing unemployment once again: by December 1991 Derwentside's dole queue had grown to 4283.

Nevertheless, job prospects in Consett are now much better than in the early 1980s. That said, many of the new jobs are low paid and relatively low skilled. To a large extent it is the sons and daughters of ex-steelworkers who have found work in the new factories making crisps, computers or engaged in light engineering and assembly; the former steelworkers themselves have not been the prime beneficiaries of the new industrial developments. Many of the new employers have wanted young labour, not the older men with traditions of unionisation, skill demarcation and relatively high pay. Moreover, while job prospects have improved, there is still a ratio of about 20 people to every registered vacancy and a large amount of unemployment concealed by government schemes. Over 2000 people in Derwentside are on the government's training and temporary employment schemes and most school-leavers go straight on to Youth Training after school - few go into jobs.

CONCLUSION

Twelve years on, it is evident that Consett has not confirmed the worst fears and expectations of the pessimists and critics. But neither has it fully recovered. As Eddie Hutchinson, the Development Agency's chief executive recently commented: 'We still have a long way to go. The unemployment rate in Derwentside is still unacceptably high.'

The Local Council is now looking ahead to the next decade and more, with plans for a massive £200 million development, financed by the public and private sectors, on the steelworks site - now given back Consett's old name, Berry Edge. It is conceived as a 'green' development, incorporating industry based on recycling, together with energy-efficient offices and housing set in a landscape of lakes and windmills generating cheap electricity. Who could have imagined a 'green' project in Consett, of all places, a decade ago?

The trauma of 'The Closure' still casts a shadow over the town and real security and prosperity remain elusive for many. 'Consett Works' still has a hollow ring about it; but Consett has, at least, survived.

FRED ROBINSON
Department of Sociology & Social Policy, University of Durham

APPENDIX I
North of England

Actual cost of erecting three blast furnaces in the north of England.

	£	s	d
Air tube	350	-	-
Boiler and masonry	500	-	-
Barrows, iron	100	-	-
Chimney	350	-	-
Cisterns, metal	300	-	-
Cages for hoist	60	-	-
Depots	850	-	-
Engine pillars, £500; engine houses, £500	1,000	-	-
Engine blowing	2,000	-	-
Engine hoist and depot	550	-	-
Boilers	1,800	-	-
Furnaces, £5000; furnace tools, £50	5,050	-	-
Furnace shells	1,214	-	-
Furnace girders	250	-	-
Heating stoves	2,500	-	-
Hoist	400	-	-
Workmen's houses, £800; office, £200	1,000	-	-
Pig beds, £150; railway, £500	650	-	-
Smith's shop	100	-	-
Slag tubs	150	-	-
Water pipes	300	-	-
Weighing machines	70	-	-
Wire rope	50	-	-
Well	250	-	-
Salaries, inspection of erections etc.	1,250	-	-
Total cost of the three furnaces	£21,094	-	-

From (Fordyce) Iron and Coal 1850 - Estimate of Building an Ironworks of the time (1840-1850).

APPENDIX II
The Mining Population

The following are extracts from the Parliamentary Commissioner's Reports, found in the Parliamentary papers of the state of the population in mining districts (1846) pp. 28-29.

A) An admirable example of wise aforethought in that particular is now being set by the newly established company, who have commenced the great undertaking of the Consett Iron Works, Shotley Bridge, Newcastle upon Tyne. This company commenced its operations in 1841, and by the end of this year (1846) their works will be the second largest in the kingdom. Their 'royalty' or right for working the minerals extends to a circle of 28 miles. Before Christmas next, they will have at work, 14 blast furnaces for smelting iron, 2 mills capable of puddling, hammering and rolling 900 tons of bar iron a week, 12 refineries for refining and founding, 22 steam engines to turn machinery, and 35 coal and ironstone pits to supply materials.

The population connected with the works will, by that time, be about 10,000! all brought together from different parts of England, Wales and Scotland, since the latter part of 1841. In addition to these, there are about 2,000 of the old rural population of the district.

Some four years later from the Parliamentary papers the state of the population in mining districts (1850) pp. 625-626.

B) Even if no sense of moral responsibility toward these 15,000! people had actuated the gentlemen who embarked in this great commercial enterprise, the lowest motives of calculation would have induced them as men of business not to expose such a vast capital without taking some security, as far as was possible, against the ignorance or misconduct of their work-people.

I know no great ironwork or other field of industry in the kingdom where so strict and conscientious a regard has been shown by the employers to the duties of their position, or where a more earnest and personal care has been devoted to everything that could contribute to the health, comfort and well being in every respect, of the labouring population.

The cottages are of the best kind, ample gardens are attached, covered drains laid down, good roads aand pathways made, good order maintained by a sufficient body of police and by strict control over the public houses, excellent schools established, libraries and other means of information and amusement encouraged, clergymen appointed, churches built, ample opportunities afforded for the religious worship of the various dissenting sects, who are always ready to organise their congregations as soon as the population begins to collect at a new spot.

The rates of wages and other details of employment are arranged on the fairest and most liberal terms, and the principles of management, as they have been on many occasions explained to me, have appeared to me to be based on a most equitable consideration for what is due to the labouring man, and to be carried into effect with strict integrity and unbending firmness.

APPENDIX III
1841 Population Census Returns, Benfieldside

In the 1841 census returns, Benfieldside is described as being 'Benfieldside that is east of the Durham and Shotley Bridge turnpike road' (now Cutlers Hall Road), and 'Benfieldside (west) that land west of the Durham to Shotley Bridge turnpike road'. Therefore the census returns give an indication of the origin of those names entered therein. In addition to the above, county of origin is denoted by a Y or N whether or nor a native of Durham County and, where indicated, region of origin was recorded.

CENSUS RETURNS 1841, BENFIELDSIDE (WEST)

Name	Occupation	Native of Co Durham Y/N	Name	Occupation	Native of Co Durham Y/N
Allison	Miner	Y	Atkinson	?	Ireland
Armstrong	Barber	N	Archer	Agric. labourer	Y
Armstrong	Papermaker	N	Atkinson	?	Y
Armstrong	Servant	Y	Aynsley		Y
Allison	Miner	N	Annandale	Independent	Scotland
Anderson	Agric. labourer	Y			
Bennet	Agric. labourer	N	Bell	Agric. labourer	Y
Beckwith	Woodsman	N	Borthwick	Millwright	Scotland
Bell	?	N	Beckwith	?	N
Bramwell	?	Y	Brabin	Farmer	Y
Bond	Servant	N	Beck	Servant	N
Burnip	Independent	N	Bertram	Servant	N
Bell	Agric. labourer	N	Bainbridge	Agric. labourer	Y
Bridge	?	Y	Barlow		Y
Boston	Chemist	N	Brown		Y
Beckwith	Gardener	Y	Briton		N
Beckwith	Woodsman	N	Bowman	?	?
Bell	Iron miner	?			
Chambers	Agric. labourer	N	Crowhall	Joiner	Y
Coulson	Mason	N	Christopher	Agric. labourer	N
Clark	?	N	Cowper	?	N
Coats	Agric. labourer	Y	Cunningham	Independent	Y
Coulson	Banker	N	Charlton	Engine Wright	Y

Name	Occupation	Native of Co Durham Y/N	Name	Occupation	Native of Co Durham Y/N
Dixon	?	Y	Dale	?	N
Duffie	?	Ireland	Dixon	?	N
Dunlop	?	Ireland	Davison		N
Emerson	Farmer	Y			
Fawcett	Quarryman	N	Fawcus	?	N
Forster	Shoemaker	N			
Graeme	Wagonman	Y	Green	Servant	N
Grimshaw	?	N	Gardiner	?	Y
Grey	Servant	N	Gibson	Farmer	Y
Graham	?	N	Garvey	Labourer	Ireland
Hall	Agric. labourer	Y	Hodgson	Grocer	Y
Harrison	Slater	Y	Henderson	Agric. labourer	N
Hall	Papermaker	Y	Hindson	Gate keeper	Y
Hawthorn	?	N	Harrison	Civil Engineer	N
Hall	?	N	Heatherington	?	Y
Hutchinson	Coachman	N	Hinds	?	N
Irwin	Joiner	N	Irwin	Tailor	N
Johnson	?	N	Johnson	?	Y
Jackson	Blacksmith	?			
Ketall	Professor of Music	N	King	Miner	
Leonard	Mason	N	Longstaff	Servant	Y
Leitch	Solicitor	N	Lindsay	?	?
Lambton	?	N	Lows	?	N
Mole	?	Y	Miller	Mason	N
Masson	?	?	Mitcheson	Labourer	
Miller	?	Ireland	Mosley	Joiner	Y
Middleton	?	N	Marshall	?	Y
Mills	?	N			
Nicholson	Agent	N	Nicholson	Agric. labourer	?
Oley	Cutler	Y	Oliver	Draper	Y

127

Name	Occupation	Native of Co Durham Y/N	Name	Occupation	Native of CoDurham Y/N
Peters	?	N	Parker	Quarryman	Y
Potts	Joiner	N	Postle	Pitman	Y
Parker	?	Y	Pallister	Papermaker	N
Potts	Servant	N	Pallister	Tinge?man?	Y
Pallister	Papermaker	N	Pallister	Blad?	?
Parry	?	N	Pattison	?	Y
Pickering	?	N			
Redshaw	Tailor	Y	Reay	Agric.Labourer	Y
Renwick	Mason	N	Ritchie	Papermaker	Ireland
Redesdale	?	Y	Reed	Draper	N
Reaney	?	Y	Ritchie	Servant	Y
Ramsey	?	Y	Robson	Independent	Y
Ramshaw	Independent	N	Reid	?	N
Richardson	?	Y	Ramshaw	Miner	Y
Richardson	?	N	Robson	?	N
Robson	Schoolmaster	N	Richardson	Farmer	N
Richardson	?	N			
Simpson	Agric. labourer	N	Selkirk	?	Y
Stephenson	?	Y	Stephenson	Labourer	Y
Stevenson	Agric. labourer	Y	Smith	Agric. labourer	Ireland
Snowdon	Mason	Y	Starling	?	?
Smith	Joiner	Y	Snowdon	Papermaker	Y
Smith	?	N	Smith	?	Y
Spencer	Servant	Y	Stout	?	N
Sewell	?	Y	Simpson	?	N
Shipley	?	N			
Thompson	Labourer	Y	Thompson	Wagonman	N
Thompson	Gardener	Y	Turbitt	Papermaker	Scotland
Turner	?	N	Thirlwell	Farmer/Butcher	Y
Thompson	?	N	Thirlwell	Servant	Y
Thompson	Coal owner	N	Thwaites	Brewer	N
Wilkinson	Mason	Y	Whitfield	Agric. labourer	N
Whaley	Labourer	Y	Waugh	?	N
Wilkinson	Papermaker	Y	Ward	Millwright	N
Williamson	?	N	Watson	Servant	Y
Walker	Blacksmith	Y	Watson	?	Y
Westgarth	Servant	N	Wheatley	?	Y

Name	Occupation	Native of Co Durham Y/N	Name	Occupation	Native of Co Durham Y/N
White	Servant	Y	Walters	Hostler	Y
Westgarth	?	N	Wood	?	N
Young	Gardener	Y			

This gave Benfieldside west 1841 census:

| No. of Houses | | | No. | No. | | av. per |
inhabited	uninhabited	buildings	male	female	total	inhab. dwelling
89	2	25	269	293	562	6.31

CENSUS RETURNS 1841, BENFIELDSIDE (EAST)

Name	Occupation	Native of Co Durham Y/N	Name	Occupation	Native of Co Durham Y/N
Askew	?	N	Anderson	Agric.labourer	N
Atkinson	Papermaker	N			
Briton	Agric. Labourer	Y	Bell	Agric. labourer	N
Bulman	Miner	Y	Brodey	Tailor and Draper	N
Black	Independent	N	Brown	Shoemaker	N
Brown	Agric.labourer	?	Bell	?	Y
Brown	Shop keeper	Y	Brook	?	N
Bell	?	Y	Brown	?	N
Brown	Agric. labourer	N	Batey	Shoemaker	Y
Bowman	Agric. labourer	N	Bell	Shoemaker	Y
Bage	Papermaker	N	Bel		Y
Cassidy	Papermaker	N	Chapman	Agric. labourer	Y
Curry	?	N	Chambers	Mason	N
Dowsey	Agric. labourer	Y	Dixon	Mason	N
Douglas	Miller	N	Davison	Agric. labourer	N
Dick	Excise Officer	N	Dixon	?	N
Dodd	?	N	Dipau	Mason	N

Name	Occupation	Native of Co Durham Y/N	Name	Occupation	Native of Co Durham Y/N
Euley	? Papermaker	N	Elliot		N
Foreman	?	N			
Garrett	?	N	Gillelly	Agric. labourer	N
Gibson	?	N			
Heads	Agric. labourer	N	Hindson	?	Y
Hall	?	Y	Henderson	Joiner	N
Houliston	Papermaker	N	Hudson	?	Y
Heslop	?	N	Hall		N
Jopling	?	N			
Kirkup	Farmer	Y	Kirsop	Agric. labourer	N
Kirkup	Cartwright	?	Kelly	Servant	Y
Lesley	?	N	Leadbitter	Agric. labourer	N
Lavery	Agric. labourer	N	Leesman	Agric. labourer	?
Lowes	Smith	Y			
Murton	Grocer	N	Moffitt	?	N
Madison	Agric. labourer	Y	Mole ?	Tailor	N
Mewes	Plasterer	N	Maudlin	?	
McGill	Agric. labourer	N	Medice	Hardware	N
Miller	Police Officer	Y			
Nicholson	?	N	Nicholson	Builder	
Newton	Stonemason?	Y			
Ord	?	N	Oley	Smith	Y
Oley	Cutler	Y	Ord	Currier	N
Oley	Cutler	Y	Oliver	Shoemaker	Y
Proud	Agric. labourer	N	Purvis	? Maker	Y
Purvis	Papermaker	Y	Parker	Agric. labourer	Y
Pickard	Brick Manufacturer	N	Price	?	N
Robinson	?	N	Routledge	?	Y
Robson	?	Y	Reardon	Roadmaker	N
Robson	Agric. labourer	N	Reoch	?	N

Name	Occupation	Native of Co Durham Y/N	Name	Occupation	Native of Co Durham Y/N
Robson	Joiner	N	Radford	Joiner	N
Robson	Miller	N	Ritson	Farmer	Y
Robson	Grocer	Y	Richardson	Farmer	Y
Routledge	Tailor	N	Ribwall	Journeyman	Y
Ritson	Saddler	Y			
Sutton	?	N	Surtees	?	Y
Surtees	Butcher	Y	Streatham	?	N
Short	Quarryman	N	Sinton	?	N
Stephenson	Agric. labourer	Y	Siddle	Currier	Y
Stephenson	? maker	Y	Sheritt	Papermaker	N
Smith	Papermaker	N	Snowball	Joiner	Y
Shadley	Coach proprietor	Y	Stirling	Pedlar	Y
Stokoe	Agric. labourer				
Todd	Miller	N	Thompson	Joiner	Y
Thompson	Papermaker	N	Toward	Engineer	Y
Thirlwell	Shoemaker	Y	Temperley	Agric.labourer	N
Virgil	Servant	N			
Wilson	?	Y	Wears	?	Y
Wardhaugh	Smith	N	Wilson	Painter	Y
Wanless	?	N	Wears	Tailor	Y
Wilkinson	Papermaker	N	Wells	Papermaker	N
Ward	?	Y	Wilson	Confectioner	N
Wilson	Painter	N	Wall	Agric. labourer	Y

Benfieldside east 1841

No. Houses inhabited	uninhabited	buildings	No. male	No. female	total	av. per inhab. dwelling
84	4	3	261	251	512	6.09

APPENDIX IV
Census Returns 1841, Conside and Knitsley

In the same 1841 census returns, the figures for Conside and Knitsley are recorded below in an alternative form, perhaps to indicate to the reader not only the size of the average household in the area, but also to indicate the age, sex, number and placement of houses at the time. The census returns of 12 June 1841, certified on the 24th of that month, gave an indication of the origin of those names entered therein.

Place	Name	Age & sex male	Age & sex female	Occupation or profession	Whether born in Co.Durham Y/N
Delves	Little Thomas	30		Blacksmith	N
"	Little Jane		25		Y
"	Little Mary		4		N
"	Little Jane		2		N
"	Little Adam	1 month			Y
"	Robson Joseph	15		Apprentice	N
"	Hutchinson Elizabeth		50	Independent	N
"	Hutchinson John	30		Agric. labourer	N
"	Wilson John	70		Agric. labourer	Y
"	Surtees Deborah		50	Independent	N
"	Surtees Robert	20		Farmer	Y
"	Surtees John	20		Coachman	Y
"	Surtees Catherine		20		Y
"	Surtees Hannah		15		Y
"	Surtees Cuthbert	65			N
"	Surtees Ann		15		Y
"	Wilson Richard	20		Agric. labourer	N
Knitsley	Hardy Robert	55		Farmer	Y
"	Hardy Margaret		45		Y
"	Hardy George	15			Y
"	Hardy Edward	13			Y
"	Hardy William	10			Y
"	Hardy Ralph	5			Y
"	Hardy Robert	15			Y
"	Hardy Mary		15	Family servant	Y
"	Reed Thomas	45		Farmer	Y
"	Reed Mary		30		Y
"	Reed Jane		6		Y
"	Reed Robert	4			Y

Place	Name	Age & sex male	female	Occupation or profession	Whether born in Co Durham Y/N
Knitsley	Reed Thomas	1			Y
"	Thompson John	25		Servant	Y
"	Thompson Luke	25		Servant	Y
"	Hall Margaret	20		Servant	Y
"	Lonsdale Margaret		15		Y
Knitsley	Dixon John	25		Agric. labourer	N
Cottage	Dixon Mary		20		N
"	Dixon Robert	1			N
Knitsley	Proud Joseph	30		Miller	Y
Mill	Proud Ann		25		Y
"	Proud Elizabeth		4		Y
"	Proud Joseph	3			Y
"	Proud Robert	8 months			Y
"	Wilson William	13		Servant	Y
"	Young Sarah		20	Servant	Y
"	Proud John	20		Agric. labourer	Y
Four Lane	Davison George	50		Inn keeper	Y
Ends	Davison Rachel		50		Y
"	Davison Robert	20		Blacksmith	Y
"	Davison Elen?		14		Y
"	Davison Mary		11		Y
Dyke Nook	Hall Jonathan	55		Farmer	Y
" "	Hall Jane	60			Y
" "	Hall John	30			Y
" "	Hall George	20			Y
" "	Hall Jane		15		Y
" "	Hall George	7			Y
" "	Thompson Thomas	25		Servant	Y
" "	Pickering Thomas	15		Servant	Y
" "	Gibson Margaret		15	Servant	Y
" "	Kirsop Jane		15	Servant	Y
" "	Appleby Henry	60		Agric. labourer	N
High	Wood Andrew	40		Agric. labourer	Y
House	Wood Mary		35		Y
"	Wood Mary		15		Y
"	Wood John	10			Y
"	Wood Hannah		5		Y
"	Wood Joseph	2			Y
Middle	Marshall Thomas	35		Farmer	Y
Gap	Marshall Ann		30		Y
"	Marshall John	20			Y

Place	Name	Age & sex male	female	Occupation or profession	Whether born in Co Durham Y/N
Middle Gap	Walton Ann		20	Servant	N
Tod Hills	Robson George	65		Joiner	Y
" "	Robson Isabel		25		Y
" "	Robson Robert	15		Apprentice	Y
" "	Rain Elizabeth		8		Y
Hounsgill	Collin William	50		Agric. labourer	Y
"	Collin Ellen		45		Y
"	Collin Jane		12		Y
"	Collin John	8			Y
"	Collin Mary		7		Y
"	Collin Catherine		4		Y
"	Collin Ellen		1		Y
"	Forman Lawrence	50		Agric. labourer	Y
The Houns	Shotton Anthony	35		Farmer	Y
" "	Shotton Margery		35		Y
" "	Shotton Thomas	1			Y
" "	Athey John	15		Servant	Y
" "	Blank Dinah		20	Servant	N
Roseyside	Bolam William	55		Woodkeeper	Y
"	Bolam Margaret		40		Y
"	Bolam Isabella		15		Y
"	Bolam Mary		2		Y
"	Bates Mabel		10		Y
Consett	Bowey William	25		Quarryman	Y
Park	Bowey Margaret		30		Y
Terrace	Bowey Mary		8 months		Y
"	Lawson Isabella		10		Y
Consett	Fleming John	25		Coalminer	Y
Park	Fleming Susan		25		Y
"	Routledge Lucy		20	Dressmaker	Y
"	Whitfield Richard	45		Farmer	Y
"	Whitfield Elizabeth		40		Y
"	Whitfield Hannah		15		Y
"	Whitfield George	10			Y
"	Whitfield William	8			Y
"	Whitfield Thomas	6			Y
"	Whitfield Phoebe		2		Y
"	Wheatley Robert	15		Servant	N
Stanford-	Taylor William	40		Farmer	Y
ham	Taylor Mary		25		Y
"	Hare Ann		20	Servant	Y

Place	Name	Age & sex male	female	Occupation or profession	Whether born in Co Durham Y/N
Stanfordham	Miller William	15			N
"	Bulman Mary		15		N
"	Bulman John	11			N
"	Bulman Joseph	10			N
"	Elliot William	30		Agric. labourer	Y
"	Jopling Thomas	50		Farmer	N
"	Jopling Elizabeth		20		Y
"	Jopling Jane		17		Y
"	Jopling Richard	20		Platelayer	Y
"	Trainer John	30		Hawker	Ireland
"	Coffrey Mary		70		Ireland
"	Green Ellen		20		Ireland
"	Poets Nancy		40	Hawker	Y
"	Mustay Barney	15		Agric. labourer	Ireland
"	Reed Joseph	15		Agric. labourer	Ireland
"	Poets Emerson	5			Y
"	McDonald John	35		Agric. labourer	Ireland
"	McDonald Mary		45		Ireland
"	not known	20		Agric. labourer	Ireland
"	not known	35		Labourer	Ireland
"	not known	20		Labourer	Ireland
"	not known	35		Labourer	Ireland
"	Jackson Matthew	45		Labourer	N
Derwent	Lister John	25		Brakeman	Y
Ironworks	Lister Margaret		25		Y
"	Lister Mary		10 months		Y
"	Smiles John	45		Labourer	Y
"	Smiles Mary		45		N
"	Smiles Mary		15		N
"	Smiles Henry		15		Y
"	Smiles Edward	12			Y
"	Smiles Margaret	8			Y
Pit House	Winter James	40		Brazer	Y
"	Winter Margery		35		N
"	Winter Phillis(spelt Filles)		15		N
"	Winter Robert	14			N
"	Winter William	10			N
"	Winter Richard	8			Y
"	Winter Mary		6		Y
"	Winter Elizabeth		4		Y
"	Winter Thomas	1			Y

Place	Name	Age & sex		Occupation or profession	Whether born in Co Durham Y/N
		male	female		
Pit House	Westgarth Joseph	40		Mason	Y
"	Westgarth Mary		40		N
"	Westgarth William	18			N
"	Westgarth Thomas	15			Y
"	Westgarth Joseph	7			Y
"	Westgarth George	1			Y
"	Gibson William	30		Labourer	Y
"	Collingwood Mary		30	Independent	Y
Consett	Hogg George	20			N
Building	Hogg Mary		20		N
"	Pears John	35		Agric. labourer	N
"	Pears Ann		25		N
"	Pears Jane	3			N
"	Pears Esther	5 months			N
"	English John	25		Labourer	N
"	Bailey Isaac	25		Labourer	N
"	Taylor Thomas	25		Gamekeeper	Y
"	Tweedy Thomas	25		Brick maker?	Y
"	Wilson William	25		Labourer	Y
"	Rof John	35		Labourer Ireland	
"	Groves George	25		Ironminer	N
"	Groves Filles?		25		N
"	Groves Thomas	4 months			Y
Consett	Wilson Christopher	30		Farmer	N
"	Wilson Ann		35		N
"	Wilson Michael	65		Servant	N
"	Hudson Margery		15	Servant	N
"	Taylor Robert	70		Farmer	Y
"	Taylor Robert	30			Y
"	Taylor Mary		35		Y
"	Taylor Ann		30		Y
"	Robson Thomas	20		Servant	Y
"	Bolam John	15		Servant	Y
"	Watson George	15		Servant	N
"	Henry Sarah		20	Servant	Y

The total given in the census returns for Conside and Knitsley (later Consett) 1841 census were:

No. of houses			No.	No.	
inhabited	uninhabited	buildings	male	female	Total
34	5		109	83	195
living in tents			1	2	

TOTALS

This gave a total for the area made up as follows:

No. of houses			No.	No.		av. per inhabited
inhabited	uninhabited	buildings	male	female	total	dwelling
BENFIELDSIDE WEST 1841						
89	2	25	269	293	562	6.31
BENFIELDSIDE EAST 1841						
84	4	3	261	251	512	6.09
CONSIDE AND KNITSLEY						
34	5		109	83	195	5.73
living in tents			1	2		
EBCHESTER (names not included)						
63	2	1	166	167	333	5.28
TOTALS						
270	13	29	806	796		

1602 people (5.93 av.)

An examination of the 1861 census returns showed the following:

No. of houses			No.	No.	av. per inhabited
inhabited	uninhabited	buildings	male	female	dwelling
BENFIELDSIDE (EAST)					
253	4	1	625	660	5.07
BENFIELDSIDE (WEST)					
169	5	-	564	426	5.85
BERRYEDGE (CONSETT)					
77	2	-	264	215	5.96
TOTAL					
499	11	1	1453	1301	

2754 (5.5 av.)

APPENDIX V
The Population of 1851 Consett

A search was undergone into the Census Returns of 1851 of Conside and Knitsley enumerators district numbers 6a (Berryedge) and 6b (Conside) of the same census. This was done to find: a) the level of employment of young children in 1851, i.e. below the age of 14 years of age at the time that the census was taken; b) the numbers of skilled and artisan classes as a percentage of the total of those living in Consett and Blackhill of 1851; c) the numbers of labouring classes as a percentage of the total of population.

CONSIDE AND KNITSLEY

ENUMERATOR'S DISTRICT 6a

No. of separate occupiers	No. of houses occupied	No. of houses uninhabited	No. houses building	Sexes M	F	Total
393	393	55	—	1297	931	2228

Average number to each household: 5.66 persons.

	No.	Per cent.
Persons working and over 14 years of age at the time of the census	414	18.581
Persons under 14 years of age	759	34.066
Labouring classes	419	18.806
Others (disabled, dependent or of independent means)	636	28.545
TOTAL	2228 persons	

Of those found to be children of under 14 years of age, 26 were registered in a number of occupations including coal miners, ironstone cleaners, labouring work and craft apprentices, and amounted to 1.16 per cent of the population.

The youngest miner listed is ten years of age, the youngest age for any boy to be allowed employment in the mines of the time. This was because of the recently passed Mines Act of 1842, which forbade such employment below that age.

ENUMERATOR'S DISTRICT 6b

No. of separate occupiers	No. of houses occupied	No. of houses uninhabited	No. houses building	Sexes M	F	Total
94	88	2	–	292	257	549

Average number to each household: 5.84 persons.

	No.	Per cent.
Persons working and over 14 years of age at the time of the census	156	28.42
Persons under 14 years of age	208	37.88
Labouring classes	69	12.57
Others (disabled, dependent or of independent means)	116	21.13
TOTAL	549 persons	

Of those found to be children of under 14 years of age, only 2 were registered as domestic servants.

Therefore from the enumerator's districts 6a and 6b of the 1851 Census returns, the total number of persons living in the town of Consett, including Delves Lane and Stanfordham Dam, was:

No. of separate occupiers	No. of houses occupied	No. of houses uninhabited	No. houses building	Sexes M	F	total
487	481	57	–	1589	1188	2777

Average number to each household: 5.70 persons.

	No.	Per cent.
Persons working and over 14 years of age at the time of the census	570	20.52
Persons under 14 years of age	967	34.82
Labouring classes	488	17.57
Others (disabled, dependent or of independent means)	752	27.07
TOTAL	2777 persons	

Of those found to be children of under 14 years of age, 28 in total were registered in work.

A complete list of the trades and occupations followed by the early residents of Consett is included, indicating their birthplace and/or town of origin. These indicate place of origin by collation into five groups:

1) Scotland 2) North of England (to include Northumberland, Durham, Westmorland, and Cumberland) 3) Yorkshire and the Midlands 4) The south west of England and Wales 5) Ireland

This was done in an effort to apportion the origins of the various settlers into the Consett area in the ten years to the time of the 1851 census.

	Number of working	Percentage of population
1) Scotland	31	5.44
2) North of England	321	56.31
3 The Midlands	47	8.24
4) The south west of England and Wales	43	7.54
5) Ireland	125	21.93
6) Others	3	0.52
TOTAL	570	

TRADES: MISCELLANEOUS, INDEPENDENT AND PROFESSIONAL

Name	Occupation	Origin
Appleby	Cow doctor	Yorkshire
Bell	Ship owner (ret.)	Northumberland
Backhouse	Independent coal-owner	Durham
Chalder	Wood bailiff and engineer	Yorkshire
Collins	Professor at day and evening school	Origin ??
Dickenson	Brick manufacturer	Durham

Name	Occupation	Origin
Fletcher	Ironmmonger	Northumberland
Grey	Retired marine customs super.	Northumberland
Gladstone	Straw bonnet-maker	Durham
Hornsby	Bookseller and newsagent	Northumberland
Murray	Auctioneer	Durham
Nesbitt	Professional missionary	Northumerland
Pattison	Independent	Northumberland
Piley	Professional railway police	Durham
Scott	Professional schoolmistress	Northumberland
Stephenson	Servant tollbar keeper	Northumberland
Sanderson	Surgeon	Edinburgh
Surtees	Independent	Shotley Bridge
Wind	Retired dragoons officer	Ireland

INNKEEPERS

Crawford	Victualler and lodge house keeper	Ireland
Dixon	Victualler beer retailer	Durham
Davison	Victualler and blacksmith	Durham
Seymour	Innkeeper	Durham
Stephenson	Victualler and barhouse keeper	Durham
Waugh	Victualler	Durham

FARMERS

Name	Acreage	Origin	Name	Acreage	Origin
Forster	20	Bishopwearmouth	Hall	?	Durham
Hardy	130	Northumberland	Hall	500	Durham
Marshall	50	Durham	Reed	190	Durham
Surtees	150	Durham	Stephenson	24	Durham
Shotton	200	Durham	Taylor	400	Northumberland
Turnbull	9	Durham	Temperley	100	Durham
Proud	76	Durham (Farmer and Miller)			
Wheatley	28	Durham (Farmer/Butcher)			

HAWKERS

Barnfather	Scotland	Gibson	Yorks
Monalin	Ireland	Mc Gowan	Ireland

GROCERS

Almond	Birtley	Ferguson	Cumberland
Fraser	Northumberland	Holiday	Cumberland
Little	Northumberland	Johnson	Northumberland

Name	Origin	Name	Origin
Kell	Durham	Potts	Durham
Postle	Durham	Surtees	Durham
Smith	Durham	White	Northumberland
Welsh	Northumberland		
Gladstone	Northumberland (Grocer and Tea dealer)		
Dickenson	Shotley Bridge (Confectioner)		
Whitfield	Durham		
Hogg	Northumberland (Greengrocer)		

BUTCHERS

Name	Origin	Name	Origin
Dickenson	Northumberland	Haywood	Shropshire
Little	Northumberland	Mares	Northumberland
March	Durham	Summerville	Northumberland
Smith (Journeyman)	Ireland	Telford	Northumberland
Waid	Durham		

DRAPERS

Name	Occupation	Origin
Gleghorn	Apprentice Draper	Northumberland
Hunter	Assistant Draper	Durham
Madlin	Draper	Northumberland
Potts	Linen and woollen Draper	Northumberland
Ross	Apprentice Draper	Durham
Sewell		Durham
Walker	Draper	Durham

TAILORS

Name	Origin	Name	Origin
Bolton	Northumberland	Bryan	Ireland
Carroll	Ireland	Clement	Durham
Davison	Northumberland	Davison	Ireland
King	Ireland	Kelly	Ireland
Nicholson	Northumberland	Quigley	Ireland
Rodden	Scotland	Rodden 12yr.old apprentice	
Scanlan	Ireland	Shanks	Durham
Warrick	Ireland		

CORDWAINERS AND BOOT MAKERS

Name	Occupation	Origin	Name	Occupation	Origin
Ball	Cordwainer	Northumberland	Ball	Cordwainer	Durham
Green	Bootmaker	Lancashire	Gibson	Master Shoe-maker	Durham

Name	Origin	Name	Origin
SHOEMAKERS			
Creddock	Durham	Dobson	Northumberland
English	Northumberland	Green	Durham
Hay	Ireland	Glennon	Northumberland
McGill	Ireland	Mowberry	Durham.
Nichol	Northumberland	Shaw	Yorks
Sewell	Durham	Whitfield	Durham
DRESSMAKERS			
Bailes	Durham	Batie	Northumberland
Bright	Durham	Clarke	Ireland
Craggs	Northumberland	Devine	Ireland
Dowson	Northumberland	Feirful?	Durham
Moir	Durham	McElhone	Ireland
Murphy	Durham	Noulan	Ireland
Parnaby	Yorks	Philipson	Durham
Proud	Durham	Robinson	Northumberland
Scott	Durham	Smiles	Durham
Sewell	Northumberland	Straine	Scotland
Turnbull	Northumberland		
SEAMSTERS			
Brown	Middlesex	Donley	Ireland
Gilhespi	Scotland	Mc Cullough	Ireland
MIDWIFES			
Hymer	Durham		

IRONMAKING INDUSTRY— BLAST FURNACE KEEPERS

Name	Origin	Name	Origin
Borans	Ireland	Cullardson	Northumberland
Elliot	Scotland	Jolsen	Northumberland
McKay	Ireland	Tilley	Durham
		(Glass furnace keeper)	

PUDDLERS

Name	Origin	Name	Origin
Berins	Lancaster	Flood	Ireland
Harris	Warwickshire	Jones	Staffordshire
Jordan	Staffordshire	Mayfield	Worcestershire
Nicholson	Yorkshire	Philipps	Shropshire
Southern	Northumberland	Smith	Yorkshire
Simpson	Yorkshire	Taylor	Durham
Westgarth	Durham	Westgarth	Cumbria

IRON REFINERS

Name	Origin	Name	Origin
Britain	Shropshire	Buttress	Lincolnshire
Buttress	North Wales	Bibbons	Lancashire

Name	Origin	Name	Origin
Bournop	Northumberland	Braun	Surrey
Birchall	Surrey	Charlton	Durham
Clifford	Derby	Cooper	Staffordshire
Crafford	Northumberland	Crafford	Northumberland
Dimmock	Staffordshire	Dunmack	Staffordshire
Dimmack	Worcester	Davis	Glamorgan
Fellows	Staffordshire	Fellow	Staffordshire
Foster	Durham	Fellowship	Staffordshire
Grant	Ireland	Geasty	Ireland
Granger	Staffordshire	Gratles	Scotland
Geutles	Durham	Gordon	Worcester
Green	Glamorgan	Gladholm	Scotland
Haris	Glamorgan	Haris	France
Harris	Staffordshire	Harley	Staffordshire
Hull	Bedfordshire	Harris	Staffordshire
Hulcutt	Scotland	Hunter	Northumberland
Irwin	Cumberland	Jackson	Yorkshire.
Jones	Flintshire	Knowles	Worcester
Little	Cumberland	Lowery	Cumberland
Longhorn	Northumberland	Longhorn	Durham
Mayfield	Worcester	Morell	Staffordshire
Malee	Staffordshire	Mc Mannon	Ireland
Mowbury	Durham	Moule	Staffordshire
McKay	Ireland	Murphy	Durham
Millhoy	Ireland	Newton	Northumberland
Newton	Staffordshire	Nicholson	Northumberland
O'Hare	Ireland	Price	Wales
Page	Shropshire	Page	Staffordshire
Perry	Durham	Philipson	Durham
Reis	Monmouth	Roberts	Monmouth
Rice	Worcester	Richards	Breconshire
Russell	Scotland	Shimmin	Isle of Man
Sterling	Northumberland	Sutton	Staffs.
Southern	Staffordshire	Stonehouse	Durham
Shaw	Staffordshire	Sutton	Shropshire
Sutton	Staffordshire	Shell	Staffordshire
Shildon	Staffordshire	Siddle	Northumberland
Swinsco	Staffordshire	Trotter	Northumberland
Thomas	Cardiganshire	Thomson	Scotland
Turley	Durham	Unsworth	Durham
Wilson	Northumberland	Wilson	Durham
Young	Yorkshire		

Name	Origin	Name	Origin
IRON ROLLERS			
Pescot	Durham	Morgan	Staffordshire
Quinton	Northumberland	Hough	Staffordshire
Jones	Worcestershire	Payne	Ireland
Murray	Ireland	White	Northumberland
Morgan	Monmouth		

Name	Origin	Name	Origin
IRON MOULDERS			
Brown	Northumberland	Grey	Scotland
Grane	Scotland	Hutchinson	Durham
Stirling	Northumberland	Lucky	Durham

Name	Occupation	Origin
SHEARSMEN		
Cornforth	Craft nail rod slitter	Staffordshire
Patterson	Boiler plate shearsman	Durham
Langstaff	Craft shearsman	Durham
Snowdon	Iron cutter	Northumberland

OTHER TRADES ASSOCIATED WITH THE IRONWORKS

ENGINEMEN (INCLUDING ENGINEERS)

Brownlee	Engineman	Durham
Burtley	Engineman	Durham
Godly	Engineer	Northumberland
Lumsden	Wagonwright	Scotland
Cameron	Engineman	Durham
Jackson	Enginewright	Durham
Patterson	Wagonwright	Cumberland
Proudlock	Engineman	Northumberland
Robson	Engineer	Northumberland
Russell	Engine driver	Durham
Sewell	Enginewright	Yorks
Todner	Engineer	Durham
Young	Engineer	Northumberland
Grey	Enginewright	Durham
Oliver	Roll turner	Bishopwearmouth
Murgrave	?	Bishopwearmouth
Lowson	Wagonwright	Cumbria
Moffitt	Boilermaker	Scotland
Wilson	Iron stoker	Durham
Henderson	Plumber/tinner	Northumberland
Young	Boilersmith	Durham

Name	Occupation	Origin
Godley	Professional Manager of rolling mills	
Wood	Foreman in rolling mill	Durham
Dixon	Railway Superintendant	Northumberland

Name	Origin	Name	Origin
BLACKSMITHS			
Bates	Durham	Blake	Scotland
Blake	Northumberland	Barrell	Durham
Bright	Durham	Clagg	Isle of Man
Connelly	Ireland	Derby	Ireland
Donelly	Ireland	Hadon	Ireland
Hubbock	Cumberland	Hubbock	Cumberland
Hall	Northumberland	Humble	Durham
Hannon	Ireland	Irwin	Cumberland
Johnson	Durham	Logan	Ireland
McFielding	Ireland	Moir	Durham
Milburn	Northumberland	McKenny	Durham
Pescot	Durham	Russell	Durham
Smith	Durham	Stoker	Northumberland
Scott	Durham	Smiles	Durham
Scott	Scotland	Turnbull	Durham
Turpin	Northumberland	Turnbull	Durham
Turnbull	Pity Me	Waters	Ireland
Whitfield	Durham		

CARPENTERS

Brinan	Ireland	Duffy	Ireland

JOINERS

Name	Origin	Name	Origin
Bailes	Durham	Dennison	Yorkshire
Moir	Scotland	Mitchell	Scotland
Sewell	Durham	Scott	Durham
Wilkinson	Northumberland		

Jackson, Cabinetmaker, Yorkshire
Hamilton, Joiner and Cartwright, Durham

Name	Occupation	Origin
STOCKTAKERS AND CLERICAL		
Archibald	Railway clerk	Durham
Brack	Clerical stocktaker in ironworks	Bishopwearmouth
Ledger	Stocktaker	Durham
Liddel	Professional agent of iron works	
Nicholson	Stocktaker in ironworks	Durham

Name	Occupation	Origin
Mules	Stocktaker	Northumberland
Thompson	Railway clerk	Durham
White	Stocktaker in ironworks	Durham

OTHERS

Name	Occupation	Origin
Elliot	Craft charcoal burner	Durham
Smith	Craft coke burner	Cumberland
Mc Gurk	Cokeburner	Ireland
Hughes	Craft at ironworks	Ireland
Finchey	Ropemaker	Ireland
Shanks	Craft brickmaker	Northumberland
Brookbanks	Craft brickmaker	Northumberland
Shield	Craft shipwright	Ireland
Caisley	Trade storekeeper	Durham
Smith	Roll tuner? or roll turner	Durham
Mathews	Forgeman	Yorkshire
Wildsmith	Forgeman	Staffordshire
Perry	Forgeman	Staffordshire
Walton	Forgeman	Yorkshire

IRONSTONE MINERS

Name	Occupation	Origin
Brians		Ireland
Cain		Ireland
Coulthard		Durham
Lindsay	14 years of age	Scotland
Moughan	Cleaning ironstone, 12 years of age	Ireland
Jacques	(retired)	Westmorland
Jacques	Appr. ironstone miner, 14 years of age	Westmorland
Proud	Iron, coal and stone miner	Durham
Smiles	Weigher of Ironstone	Durham

Name	Origin
LEAD MINER	
Price	Northumberland

Name	Origin	Name	Origin
STONE MASONS			
Allison	Durham	Casson	Cumbria
Coulters	Yorkshire	Dixon	Northumberland
Dufton	Northumberland	Hornsby	Northumberland
Kenna	Ireland	Kell	Durham
		(Mason and quarryman)	
Lose	Durham	Mc Glone	Ireland
Ross	Durham	Shorlen	Ireland

Name	Origin	Name	Origin
Westgarth	Durham	Walsh	Ireland
Westgarth	Shotley Bridge		

COAL MINERS

Name	Origin	Name	Origin
Armstrong	Scotland	Anderson	Durham
Anderson	Cumberland	Anderson	Ireland
Anderson	Durham	Atkinson	Northumberland
Agnew	Ireland		
Bell	Northumberland	Bulmer	Ireland
Brians	Ireland	Bell	Scotland
Brown	Northumberland	Burtley	Durham
Brook	Northumberland	Brook	Durham
Clark	Northumberland	Craggs	Durham
Conkinson	Scotland	Cockley	Cumberland
Conney	Ireland	Corcoran	Ireland
Campbell	Ireland	Collison	Durham
Cunningham	Ireland	Corran	Ireland
Charlton	Durham	Cummins	Ireland
Corrigan	Ireland	Calvert	Durham
Curry	Durham	Crister	Durham
Coleman	Ireland	Connolly	Ireland
Core	Ireland	Crowther	Norfolk
Cameron	Cumberland	Cameron (13yrs)	Cumberland
Cartey	Lancaster	Cameron	Cumberland
Durberry	Cumberland	Donnelly	Ireland
Dagleish	Durham	Dodson	Northumberland
Dodson (14yrs)	Northumberland	Dodds	Northumberland
Dover	Westmorland	Dolan	Ireland
Ebbet	Ireland		
Fielding	Ireland	Fantarrow	Northumberland
Fitzsimmons	Ireland		
Gladden	Yorkshire	Gladholm	Cumberland
Garling	Ireland	Glenwright	Northumberland
Galmay	Ireland		
Holmes	Northumberland	Handling	Ireland
Heslop	Northumberland	Hodger	Ireland
Heatherington	Northumberland	Heatherington	Durham

Name	Origin	Name	Origin
Hymer	Durham	Hanlon	Ireland
Hand (14 yrs) (Driver in coal pit)	Ireland	Irwin	Durham
Jacques	Westmorland	Johnson (10 yrs)	Durham
Kelly	Ireland	Kelly	Ireland
Lewson	Ireland	Little	Cumberland
Liddle	Yorkshire	Ladler	Durham
Liddle	Durham	Lochran	Ireland
Lawson	Ireland		
Martin	Ireland	Munaghan	Ireland
Miller	Scotland	McDonald	Ireland
Maddison	Durham	Maddison	Northumberland
Moore	Yorkshire	McCristle	Ireland
McMahon	Ireland	McEray	Ireland
McCardill	Ireland	McMannis	Ireland
McKenna	Ireland	McGovern	Ireland
McGee	Ireland	McGain	Ireland
McCullum	Scotland	McKenson	Ireland
McWilliams	Ireland	Mastin	Ireland
Murphy	Ireland	Mc Donald	Ireland
Margin	Ireland	McKene	Ireland
Nicholson	Northumberland		
Parnaby	Yorkshire	Parker	Northumberland
Purvis	Durham	Purvis (11 yrs)	Durham
Philipson	Durham		
Quin	Ireland		
Rhynes	Ireland	Rogan	Ireland
Stephenson	Durham	Scott	Scotland
Strong	Durham	Smailes	Durham
Smith	Ireland	Stephenson	Durham
Smith	Northumberland	Smyth	Ireland
Smith	Ireland	Sweeney	Ireland
Shriden	Ireland	Smith	Hampshire

Name	Origin	Name	Origin
Taite	Northumberland	Thorburn	Durham
Turnbull	Northumberland	Tiddis	Northumberland
Walton	Cumberland	Walton (14 yrs)	Cumberland
Williams	Devon	Williams	Staffordshire
Willis	Durham	Walsh	Ireland

SERVANTS

Name	Origin	Name	Origin
Best	Northumberland	Brown	Durham
Blair	Durham		
Carnaby	Northumberland	Cragg	Durham
Crawford	Ireland	Calver	Durham
Cartey	Ireland	Douglas	Northumberland
Eliott	Durham	Grey	Essex
Henderson	Durham	Halfpenny	Ireland
Hardy	Durham	Iceton	Durham
Johnson	Durham	Leiton	Northumberland
Lowther	Northumberland	Little	Northumberland
McGill	Ireland	Moralee	Durham
McLoon	Ireland	Milburn	Northumberland
McMillan	Northumberland	Oliver	Northumberland
Ross	Durham	Patterson	Northumberland
Robinson	Scotland		
Stoker	Northumberland	Samen	Ireland
Stobbs	Durham	Stephenson	Staffordshire
Telford	Cumbria	Turnbull	Durham
Urwin	Durham		
Watson	Durham		

WASHER WOMEN

Name	Origin	Name	Origin
Calmoor	Durham	Morgan	Ireland
McAnally	Ireland	Ramsay	Northumberland

Name	Occupation	Origin
OTHERS		
Bolam	Retired Husbandman	Durham
Bates	Housekeeper	Durham
Blades	Hairdresser	Yorkshire
Craggs	Slater	Durham
Dobson	Rail engineman	Durham
Dodsworth	Farmers hinde	Yorkshire
Frazer	Traveller	Scotland
Haggeston	Stagecoach-driver	Durham
Haggeston	Stagecoach-servant	Durham
Moffitt	Florist	Scotlamnd
Mc Cluskey		Ireland
Oates	Weaver	Ireland
Rutherford	Head Sawyer	Northumberland
Swinbank	Farmers Hinde	Durham
Thorburn	Shepherd	Scotland
Trainer	Gardener	Ireland
Turnbull	Platelayer	Northumberland
Ward	Weaver	Ireland
Westgarth	Cartman	Durham
Waugh	Platelayer	Northumberland

Addendum

AGRICULTURAL WORKERS

The average weekly earnings of an agricultural worker in the mid-nineteenth century was about ten shillings a week. Any overplus (overtime?) time was set aside to pay the rent. Meals were coffee made very weak to breakfast. Dine on bacon, fry and potatoes. To sup on, tea. The labourer did not go home to dinner, but took bacon and a piece of bread with him into the field and a mug of milk.

APPENDIX VI
Population Census of 1851, Blackhill

A further search was undergone into the census returns of 1851 of Benfieldside, enumerator's district numbers 4a and 4b. This was done to determine:

a)   the level of employment of young children in 1851 i.e. below the age of 14 years of age at the time that the census was taken.

b)   the numbers of skilled and artisan classes as a percentage of the total of those living in Blackhill in 1851.

c)   the numbers of labouring classes as a percentage of the total of population.

The investigation also took into account the amended figure of the district 4a, as the portion of the 1851 census of that district included all that portion of the township of Benfieldside which has to the north of the turnpike road leading from Lanchester to Shotley Bridge, excluding all of the enumeration district except those registered as being in Blackhill; and the total of district 4b, which included all that part of Benfieldside which lay to the south of the Lanchester to Shotley Bridge turnpike road (modern day Durham Road, Blackhill), excepting Shotley Grove, Bridgehill and Howden. These areas were excluded from the survey as it was felt that they were too far removed from and remote from the proximity of the populations and industries of early Blackhill.

From the complete enumerator's district 4a (Benfieldside) the 1851 census returns show:

No of separate occupiers	No of houses occupied	No of houses uninhabited	No. of buildings	Sexes M	F	Total
281	271	13	–	696	726	1422

Therefore the average number of persons per dwelling was 5.06 persons. The amended figures i.e. to exclude all enumerator's district 4a excepting those registered in Blackhill are then seen as:

No of separate occupiers	No of houses occupied	No of houses uninhabited	No. of buildings	Sexes M	F	Total
49	49	–	–	116	101	217

Average number of persons per dwelling: 4.28.
From the same census the following was also arrived at:

	No.	Percent. of total
Persons working and over 14 years of age at the time of the census	62	28.57
Persons under 14 years of age	69	31.79
Labouring classes	31	14.28
Others (disabled, dependent or of independent means)	55	25.34

TOTAL   217

Of those under 14 years of age, only three were registered as working.

From the complete enumerator's district 4b (Benfieldside) the 1851 census returns show:

No. of separate occupiers	No. of houses occupied	No. of houses uninhabited	No. of buildings	Sexes		Total
				M	F	
174	174	103	–	586	467	1053

Average number of persons per dwelling: 6.05.

The amended figures for the investigation, i.e. excluding Shotley Grove, Bridgehill and Howden from the survey are then seen as:

No. of separate occupiers	No. of houses occupied	No of houses uninhabited	No. of buildings	Sexes		Total
				M	F	
155	155	103	–	537	414	951

Average number of persons per dwelling: 6.13.

From the amended enumerator's district 4b Benfieldside the following numbers also become evident:-

	No.	Percent. of total
Persons working and over 14 years of age at the time of the census	161	16.92
Persons under 14 years of age	346	36.38
Labouring classes	210	22.08
Others (disabled, dependent or of independent means)	234	24.60

TOTAL   951

Of those under 14 years of age, eight were as registered as working.

The Mines Act of 1842 forbade anyone younger than ten years of age to be employed underground.

By adding together both of the amended tables of both enumerators' districts 4a and 4b, a more complete statistical picture can be gained of the Blackhill of 1851:

No. of separate occupiers	No. of houses occupied	No. of houses uninhabited	No. of buildings	Sexes		Total
				M	F	
204	204	103		653	515	1168

Average number of persons per dwelling: 5.7.

From the same census the following is arrived at:

	No.	Percentage of total
Persons working and over 14 years of age at the time of the census	223	19.09
Persons under 14 years of age	415	35.53
Labouring classes	241	20.63
Others (disabled, dependent or of independent means)	289	4.74

TOTAL 1168

Of those under 14 years of age, only eleven were registered as working, amounting to 0.94 per cent of the entire population of Blackhill.

Of all workers, 178 were recorded in a great range of occupations. A list of the traders and occupations followed by the early residents of Blackhill, indicating their birthplace and or town of origin, follows.

	No. recorded	Percentage of total
Scotland	11	5.18
North of England (Northumberland, Durham, Cumberland and Westmorland)	102	57.30
Yorkshire and the Midlands	19	10.67
The south west and Wales	13	7.30
Ireland	31	17.41
Others	2	1.12

TOTAL 178

PROFESSIONAL AND TRADING NAMES BLACKHILL 1851

Name	Occupation	Origin
Christopher	Farmer	Durham
Cundle	Schoolteacher	Northumberland
Chambers	Police officer	Scotland
Clark	Teacher	Durham
Collin	Schoolmaster	Ireland
Darley	Schoolteacher	Isle of Man
Forbes	Schoolteacher	Northumberland
Rankin	Teacher	Northumberland
Proud	Veterinary surgeon	Durham
Jones	Teacher of needlework	Northumberland
Thompson	Draughtsman	Northumberland

INNKEEPERS

Name	Occupation	Origin
Douglas	Beerhouse keeper	Northumberland
Moore	Innkeeper	Leicestershire
Wigham	Trade brewer	Durham
Kerry	Domestic ostler	Ireland

OTHERS

Name	Occupation	Origin
Ainslie	Wood agent	Durham
Burnope	Cartman	Northumberland
Bowman	Straw hat maker	Cumberland
Chapman	Apprentice	Durham
Dixon	Shopman	Yorkshire
Foreman	Baker	Northumberland
Harrison	Ironmonger	Durham
Japes	Sawyer	Northumberland
Mullen	Dealer	Ireland
Mcgrane	Rag gatherer	Ireland
Newsmastch	Tallow chandler	Middlesex
O'Neal	Dealer	Ireland
Ord	Ironmonger	Northumberland
Park	Sawyer	Scotland
Skelton	Toll collector	Yorkshire
Souter	Wagonman	Scotland
Wilkinson	Straw hat maker	Ebchester
Wherle	Craft clock maker	Germany
Thompson	Chemist, druggist and stationer	Durham

Name	Origin	Name	Origin

DOMESTIC SERVANTS

Clarke	Northumberland	Parker	??
Hayman	Scotland	McLenson	Northumberland
Thompson	Durham	Armstrong	Northumberland
Farley, Husbandry servant, Ireland		Thompson	Durham
Busby, Saddler	Northumberland	Busby, Groom	Cumberland

TAILORS AND ASSOCIATED TRADES

Usher	Northumberland	Spencer, Tailor and Draper, Durham	
Walton	Northumberland	Turner	Northumberland
Stringer	Durham	Male	Shotley Bridge
Routledge	Durham	Heatherington, Draper, Cumberland	
Kennedy, Weaver	Scotland		

GROCERS AND BUTCHERS

Belldon	Northumberland	Bell	Slaley
Graydon	Northumberland	Mewes	Northumberland
Richardson	Durham	Barkas, Grocer and Draper,Durham	
Collinson, Grocer and Draper, Durham			

BUTCHERS

Lovatt	Northumberland	Ainsley	Scotland
Todd, Butcher and Grocer, Cumberland			

DRESSMAKERS

Mohan	Ireland	Stringer	Yorkshire
Ward	Northumberland	Usher	Northumberland
Bulmen	Cumberland	Ridley	Yorkshire
Archer, Milliner	Cumberland		

SHOEMAKERS

Cook	Northumberland	Campbell	Ireland
Mountain	Ireland	Watson	Durham
Bell	Northumberland	Baty	Northumberland
Richley, Cordwainer, Northumberland		Dodgon, Cordwainer, Durham	
Rickley, Leather cutter, Northumberland			

Ironmakers and Associated Trades

PUDDLERS

Brodie	Northumberland	Conroy	Ireland
Foster	Northumberland	Grayson	Northumberland
Glancy	Ireland	Hammel	Ireland
Henderson	Northumberland	Murphy	Scotland
Murphy	Northumberland	MaLean	Ireland

Name	Origin	Name	Origin
Shenan	Ireland	Simpson	Scotland
Telford	Cumberland	Timney	Ireland

BOILER PLATE ROLLERS

Name	Origin	Name	Origin
Butler	Worcester	Holiday	Staffordshire
Butler	Staffordshire		
	+ three sons (same work)		

Name	Occupation	Origin

TINPLATE MAKERS

Name	Occupation	Origin
Brodie	Craft tin-roller	Northumberland
Coslett	Roller of tinplate	Monmouth
Harris	Tinplate furnaceman	Staffordshire
Malpass	Roller of tinplate	Glamorgan
Malpass	Tinplate doubler	Worcester
Malpass	Tinplate furnaceman	Worcester
Maxwell	Craft whitesmith	Northumberland
Nicholas	Washman of tinplate	Wales
Rees	Craft nailer of tinplates	Monmouth
Winmill	Pickler of tin	Glamorgan
Winmill	Manager of tinplate works	Glamorgan
Winmill	Tinman	Monmouth

COAL MINERS BLACKHILL 1851

Name	Origin	Name	Origin
Bell	Durham	Bewley	Cumberland
Burnope	Northumberland	Bewley	Cumberland
Christie	Scotland	Coals	Northumberland
Callan	Ireland	Calvin	Northumberland
Carr	Scotland	Featherson	Durham
French	Northumberland	Feather	Durham
Guin	Ireland	Guin	Northumberland
Guin (10 yrs)	Ireland	Halpin	Ireland
Japes	Durham	Jackson	Durham
McNally	Ireland	McNally	Ireland
McKensie	Scotland	Martin	Ireland
Simpson	Northumberland	Simpson	Durham
Turner	Scotland	Thorp	Lancashire
Walton	Durham	Mohan (10 yrs)	Ireland

IRONSTONE MINERS

Name	Origin	Name	Origin
Blake	Ireland	Burns	Ireland
Marrin	Ireland	Malone	Ireland

BLACKSMITHS

Name	Origin	Name	Origin
Apple	Yorkshire	Chilton	Durham
Eggleston	Durham	Hope	Durham

Name	Origin	Name	Origin
Lockley	Durham	Wetherall	Yorkshire
Farley	Ireland	Jackson	Northumberland
Jackson	Northumberland	Robson	Northumberland

MASONS

Name	Origin	Name	Origin
Barber	Northumberland	Simpson	Durham
Wilkinson	Durham	Finnegan	Ireland
Christopher	Durham	Soulsby, Mason	Yorkshire
Gray	Craft mason and beerhouse keeper		Northumberland

Name	Occupation	Origin

ENGINE MEN

Name	Occupation	Origin
Ragg	Colliery engineman	Durham
Gardiner	Engineman	Durham
Appleby	Servant fireman	
Thompson	Engine fitter	Ireland

OTHERS

Name	Occupation	Origin
Blenkhorn	Roll turner	Yorkshire
Dodd	Coke burner	Northumberland
Foster	Joiner	Northumberland
Gardiner	Foreman	Durham
Hope	Craft nailer	Durham
Marshall	Nailmaker	Durham
Henderson	Cleric stocktaker	Northumberland
Nicholas	Weigher of iron	Northumberland
Patterson	Craft shearsman	Northumberland
Rimmer	Joiner	Lancashire
Thompson	Colliery joiner	Northumberland
Temprley	Cleric at ironworks	Northumberland
Sawers	Forgeman	Northumberland
Sowers	Forgeman	Durham
Sawers	Apprentice forgeman	Durham
Mansell	Mill furnaceman	Staffordshire
Taylor	Patternmaker	Staffordshire
Humphries	Millwright	Wales
Jameson	Millwright	Northumberland
Spinner	Craft nailer	Ireland
Ridley	Pipemaker	Northumberland
Nichol	Craft forgeman	Staffordshire

In the collation and recording of the above, some titles of work and names and places of origin have been omitted solely to avoid repetition.

APPENDIX VII
Average Selling Prices of Tin

(Shillings per box of 225 sheets $13^3/_4$" x 10", weight 1 cwt.)

Year	Tinplate		Tin (per ton)		
1849	27s.	6d.	£77.	8s.	4d.
1850	27s.	4d.	£76.	15s.	0d.
1851	25s.	3d.	£81.	15s.	0d.
1852	23s.	2d.	£84.	6s.	8d.
1853	25s.	9d.	£111.	11s.	8d.
1854	26s.	10d.	£116.	0s.	0d.
1855	26s.	11d.	£114.	6s.	8d.
1856	30s.	5d.	£132.	5s.	0d.
1857	32s.	3d.	£137.	1s.	8d.
1858	25s.	10d.	£116.	0s.	0d.
1859	25s.	6d.	£132.	11s.	8d.
1860	24s.	4d.	£131.	5s.	0d.
1861	21s.	7d.	£119.	5s.	0d.
1862	21s.	4d.	£116.	0s.	0d.
1863	21s.	10d.	£120.	10s.	0d.
1864	23s.	7d.	£106.	1s.	8d.
1865	22s.	5d.	£92.	5s.	0d.
1866	25s.	0d.	£82.	1s.	0d.

From the Monograph of *Tinplate Works* by E. H. Brooke.

APPENDIX VIII
Monthly Prices of Tinplate 1827-1850

(Shillings per box of 225 sheets 13³/₄" x 10", weight 1 cwt.)

	Jan.	Feb.	Mar.	Apr.	May	June	July	Aug.	Sept.	Oct.	Nov.	Dec.
1827	42	42	42	42	40	40	40	38	38	40	40	40
1828	40.5	40.5	40.5	40.5	38	38	38	38	38	37	37	37
1829	37	40	40	40	39	38	37	36	35	34	34	34
1830	34	34	38	32.5	32.5	32.5	32.5	32.5	32.5	32.5	32.5	32.5
1831	32.5	32.5	32.5	32	32	32	33	33	33	32	32	32
1832	31.5	31	31	31	31	30	30	30	30	30	30	30
1833	30	30	30	32	32	32	32	32	32	32	36	36
1834	36	36	38	38	38	38	37	37	37	35	35	35
1835	35	35	35	35	35	35	35	35	35	35	35	38
1836	38	44	44	44	44	44	47	47	47	45	45	44
1837	42	40	40	36	35	34	33	32	33.5	34	33.5	33.5
1838	33	33	33	36	36	34	33.5	31.5	31.5	34	34	34
1839	33	35	34.5	33	33.5	33.5	33	33	33	33	33	33
1840	33	33	33	33	32	32	32	34	34	34	33	31.5
1841	32	31	33	32	32.5	32.5	32	32	32	32	32	32
1842	32	32	32	32	32	31	30	29	28	28.5	28.2	27.5
1843	27.5	27	27	26.5	25.8	25.8	25.2	25.5	25	25.2	26.5	25.5
1844	25.2	26	27	26.5	30	30.5	30.2	30.2	30	28.5	28.5	28.5
1845	28	29	32	35	34	33	33	29.2	29.2	30.5	32.5	32
1846	31	30.5	29	29	28	28	28	27.8	28	28	28.5	28.5
1847	30	29.5	29.5	28.5	28.5	28.5	27.5	27.5	27.5	27.5	27.5	27
1848	26.5	26.5	26.5	26.5	26.5	26	25.8	25.8	25.5	26.5	26.5	27.5
1849	27.5	27.5	30	31	29	28	26.5	26.8	27.5	28.2	27.2	27.8
1850	29.8	28.8	28.2	27.2	26.8	26.5	27.2	28	28	27.5	27.5	27.5